Mystery Handy Helpers

Use the clues to solve these riddles about hand-held helpers. Complete each drawing.

1. Your bathroom is probably my home. I help you have a healthy smile.	2. Find me in a desk or drawer. Handle me with care because my points are sharp.
3. In the kitchen I'll be found. Look for me when it's time to eat.	4. You always seem to be looking for me when you need to jot something down.
5. A rip or a hole I'll help you mend, along with my friend, thread. 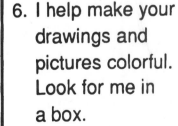	6. I help make your drawings and pictures colorful. Look for me in a box.

Try This! Create a mystery picture and riddle for a friend to solve.

Read the story. Write a word from the Word Box to complete each sentence.

Word Box

sleepy   excited   angry

confused   sad

1. "My birthday is finally here," Scott said. "Now I can open the big package that is on the kitchen table."
Scott is feeling

_____ .

2. Meg wanted to see the end of the movie. Her eyes kept closing. She yawned over and over. It was getting late.
Meg was very

_____ .

3. The little boy's mother grabbed his hand. She pointed at the cars rushing by. She told him in a loud voice that he must stay with her.
The boy's mother is

_____ .

4. Mark is not sure which way to go. He thinks the playground is nearby. He hopes to see someone he knows who can help him.
Mark is

_____ .

5. Ann wished her friend had not moved. She thought about her every day. She hoped they could be together again soon.
Ann is feeling

_____ .

Brainwork! Draw a face to illustrate each word in the Word Box. Write the word under each face.

2

Read the story. Write **true** or **false** by each sentence about the story.

1. The teacher asked the students to get their coats. Then the students lined up by the door. The teacher reminded everyone to bring an egg carton to school tomorrow for a special art lesson.

   a. _____ The class was getting ready for school to begin.

   b. _____ The class was ready to go home.

   c. _____ They are going to use egg cartons at school.

   d. _____ It was time for a reading lesson.

2. The hamster looked in the dish. Then he ran around the cage. He put his nose to the glass when we came near. When we put food in the dish, he started eating.

   a. _____ The hamster was very sleepy.

   b. _____ The hamster was getting out of the cage.

   c. _____ The hamster was hungry.

   d. _____ The hamster was awake.

3. Beth and Meg read the recipe. They put everything in the big bowl and mixed it together. Dad turned on the oven. The girls put spoonfuls of the batter on cookie sheets. They had Dad put the cookies into the oven.

   a. _____ Beth and Meg are making the cookies without help.

   b. _____ The girls work well together.

   c. _____ Beth and Meg work safely in the kitchen.

   d. _____ Beth and Meg did not have all the ingredients they needed.

Brainwork! Write five true or false statements about yourself. Ask a friend to read them and tell if they are true or false.

Do's and Don'ts

The *do's* and *don'ts* below describe common objects you might see at home. Use the clues to find out what's being described. Write the correct word on the line and color its picture.

1. I do have a plug.
   I don't make noise.
   I am a _____ .

TV

lamp

2. I do have legs.
   You don't sit on me.
   I am a _____ .

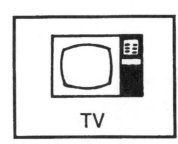
table

chair

3. I do open and close.
   You don't walk through me.
   I am a _____ .

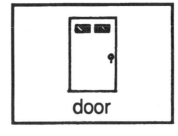
door

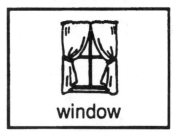
window

4. I do hold water.
   You don't take a bath in me.
   I am a _____ .

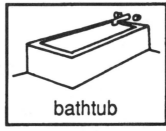
bathtub

sink

5. I do go on your feet.
   I don't leave the house.
   I am _____ .

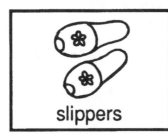
slippers

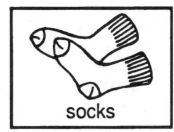
socks

Try This! Choose an object that you see in your classroom. Describe it with *do's* and *don'ts*. Have a friend guess the object.

4

What Next?

Read the sentences about each picture. Decide what is *most likely* to happen next. Write your choice on the line.

1. The cake was finally cool. Bill got the knife and bowl of icing. What will happen next?

   • Bill will cut the cake.
   • Bill will spread the icing.

   _____

2. The sky became dark. Mark heard rumbling and saw flashes of light. What will happen next?

   • It will begin to rain.
   • The power will go out.

   _____

3. Tasha tossed the stick across the yard. Shaggy ran to get it. What will happen next?

   • Shaggy will bring it back to Tasha.
   • Tasha will toss a ball across the yard.

   _____

4. Mother Bird returned to her nest with a juicy worm. The babies' mouths were open. What will happen next?

   • Mother will eat the worm.
   • Mother will feed her babies.

   _____

Try This! For one of the stories above, write why you chose your answer.

It Isn't

In each box below you are to find out what animal is described. One way to do this is by first deciding what animal it *isn't*. Read the clues. Use each animal's name only once to complete the sentences. Then follow the directions.

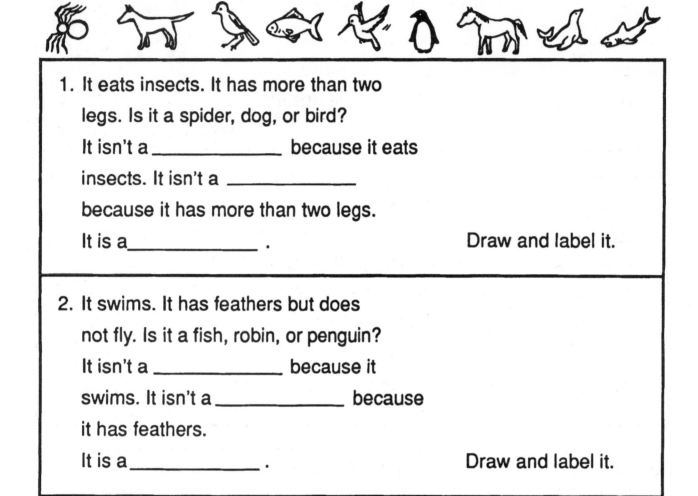

1. It eats insects. It has more than two
   legs. Is it a spider, dog, or bird?
   It isn't a _____ because it eats
   insects. It isn't a _____
   because it has more than two legs.
   It is a_____ .   Draw and label it.

2. It swims. It has feathers but does
   not fly. Is it a fish, robin, or penguin?
   It isn't a _____ because it
   swims. It isn't a _____ because
   it has feathers.
   It is a_____ .   Draw and label it.

3. It is covered with hair. It lives in the
   sea. Is it a horse, seal, or shark?
   It isn't a _____ because it's
   covered with hair. It isn't a _____
   because it lives in the sea.
   It is a _____ .   Draw and label it.

Try This! Create your own *It Isn't* riddle for a friend to solve.

Read the story. Write **true** or **false** by each sentence about the story.

1. Jeff wanted a pet. He went to the library to get out a book on cats. He wanted to find out how to take care of a kitten. Then he and his family would go to the animal shelter to get a kitten.

   a. _____ Jeff does not know if he wants a cat or dog.

   b. _____ Jeff wants to learn about kittens.

   c. _____ Jeff went to the pet store.

   d. _____ Jeff found a cat at the library.

2. Peter is glad the tree is big and strong. He wants to build a tree fort in it. Daddy will buy the wood for the fort early Saturday morning. Then they will start working on the fort.

   a. _____ Peter hopes it rains Saturday.

   b. _____ The tree was planted last week.

   c. _____ The fort will be made of wood.

   d. _____ Peter is building the fort by himself.

3. Cindi was looking forward to Friday night. She would use her new sleeping bag. She knew it was going to be fun staying at her best friend's house. She wondered what they would have for breakfast in the morning.

   a. _____ Cindi is going camping.

   b. _____ The sleeping bag has never been used.

   c. _____ Cindi will stay overnight with her friend.

   d. _____ Cindi will be at her friend's house on Saturday morning.

Brainwork! Make a list of things Cindi will take to her friend's house.

Read the clues. Write the answer on the line.

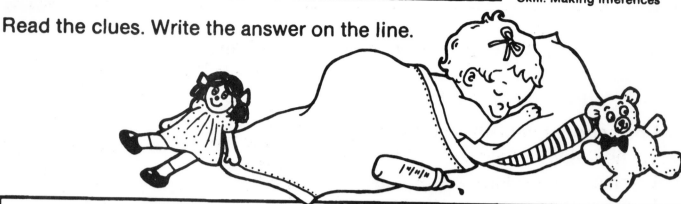

1. I sleep in a crib.
   I drink from a bottle.
   I cannot walk or talk.
   Who am I?

   _____

   a puppy, a baby, a clown

2. Put me on your feet.
   I will keep you warm and dry.
   Wear me when it rains.
   What am I?

   _____

   socks, shoes, boots

3. I grow on an ear.
   Cook me in hot oil.
   I will puff up and taste good.
   What am I?

   _____

   French fries, popcorn,
   a hot dog

4. Paste me on an envelope.
   You need me before you can
   mail a letter.
   What am I?

   _____

   a mailbox, a post card,
   a stamp

5. I have no color.
   You need me every day.
   You drink me when you are
   thirsty.
   What am I?

   _____

   juice, water, milk

6. I look like a baby.
   You can give me a name.
   Children like to play with me.
   What am I?

   _____

   a teddy bear, a doll, a ball

Brainwork! Write clues about an object. Ask a friend to guess the
name of the object.

Read the story. Write the answers to the questions.

The Talent Show

The school talent show was going to be held again. Pam and Patti both circled the date on their calendars.

Pam practiced playing piano every day. Patti did her dance for the show over and over. She showed the dance to Pam at school on the playground.

The girls' families will get there early so that they can find seats in the front row. Last year at the end of the show, the audience clapped and cheered.

1. You can tell that the girls probably attended the same school because

   _____ .

2. Why do you think there will be a lot of people watching the show?

   _____

3. The reason Pam and Patti are practicing so much is _____

   _____ .

4. When the girls found out about the show, they probably felt
   (silly, frightened, excited) _____ .

5. Before Patti dances at the show, she will probably be feeling
   (proud, nervous, angry) _____ .

6. What clue word tells you the show has been held before?

   _____

Brainwork! Make a picture about a school talent show.

Read the story and the two sentences after the story. Write the **true** sentence on the line.

1. Emily looked at the list. She put her things in the suitcase. She was happy that her friend was going with her. She knew they would have fun swimming, fishing and sleeping in a tent.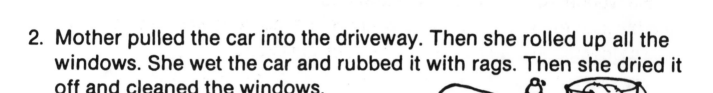

    a. Emily is going to school.
    b. She is going to camp.

    _____

2. Mother pulled the car into the driveway. Then she rolled up all the windows. She wet the car and rubbed it with rags. Then she dried it off and cleaned the windows.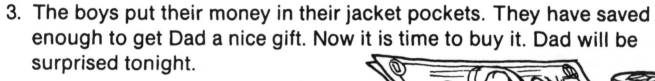

    a. Mother has a new car.
    b. She washed the car.

    _____

3. The boys put their money in their jacket pockets. They have saved enough to get Dad a nice gift. Now it is time to buy it. Dad will be surprised tonight.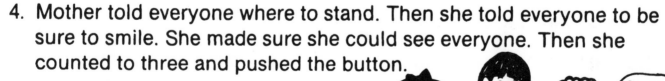

    a. The boys are going shopping.
    b. The boys will get their favorite toys.

    _____

4. Mother told everyone where to stand. Then she told everyone to be sure to smile. She made sure she could see everyone. Then she counted to three and pushed the button.

    a. Mother took a picture.
    b. Mother needs new glasses.

    _____

Brainwork! Draw and label five things the boys might buy for Dad.

 FS-32028 Critical Thinking

Can You Tell?

Read the story and statements below carefully. Decide if each statement is true, false, or if you can't tell from the information given in the story. Fill in the correct circle beside each statement.

A Fresh Start

Greg was moving to a new town on September 4, just in time to start the year in a new school.

He wondered if he would be allowed to ride his bike to this school. He was too young last year. In his last school, only students ten or older could ride bikes to school.

He wondered who his new friends would be. Would they want to watch TV after school, or would they rather play outside like he does?

Greg's brother would be going to the same school. Greg decided they could help each other make new friends.

		True	False	Can't Tell
1. Greg will move in before school starts.	1.	○	○	○
2. Greg is ten years old.	2.	○	○	○
3. Greg would rather watch TV after school than play outside.	3.	○	○	○
4. Greg has an older brother.	4.	○	○	○
5. Greg rode his bike to school last year.	5.	○	○	○
6. Greg's new school starts in September.	6.	○	○	○
7. Greg is in third grade.	7.	○	○	○
8. Greg would like to ride his bike to school.	8.	○	○	○

Try This! Based on the story, write how you think Greg feels about moving.

Read the story. Write the answers to the questions.

Faraway Friends

Jane hoped to get another letter from Kim soon. Kim was in third grade also. Kim promised she would send a photograph of herself. It was fun to hear from someone who was living on an island in the United States where the weather is always warm. Jane wondered if Kim would like to play in the snow in her backyard in Michigan. Jane hoped that someday she would get to meet her faraway friend.

4100

1. You can tell the girls are about the same age because _____

_____.

2. Jane wants to see Kim's photograph because she is probably

wondering _____.

3. What clue word tells you that Jane has received other letters

from Kim? _____.

4. What clue word tells you that Jane is in third grade? _____

5. Kim probably lives in (Bermuda, Hawaii, Arizona) _____.

6. If Jane does not get a letter soon, she probably will be feeling

(excited, disappointed, nervous) _____.

Brainwork! Write what it might be like to play in snow for the first time.

 FS-32028 Critical Thinking

Name _____

Read the story and the two sentences after the story. Write the **true** sentence on the line.

1. The air is warm. Birds are singing in the morning. The grass is growing again. Flowers are starting to pop out of the ground. Soon days will be much longer.

   a. Spring is here.
   b. It is a hot summer day.

   _____

2. It was a special day in October. Beth made a jack-o-lantern. She put on her costume and carried a big bag. Then her mother took her to different houses. When she came home, she had candy in her bag.

   a. Beth went to a Halloween party.
   b. Beth went trick or treating.

   _____

3. Matt used a crayon to write his name on the bag. He made a peanut-butter-and-jelly sandwich and put it in the bag. He put in an apple and three cookies. Then he folded the top of the bag.

   a. Matt is hungry.
   b. Matt is packing his lunch.

   _____

4. Sara telephoned her friend. She told her what happened at school that day. She said she hoped she would be at school tomorrow.

   a. Sara's friend moved away.
   b. Her friend was absent.

   _____

Brainwork! Draw a picture of one of the sentences that was false on this page.

Name _____

Read the story. Write a word from the
Word Box to complete each sentence.

Word Box
tiny   brave
hungry   shy
    frightened

1. Emily woke up early. She
   worried that her new school
   would be different. She hoped
   the teacher would ask
   someone to be her special
   friend today.
   Emily is a

   _____ person.

2. Brian could hear loud cracks of
   thunder. He could hear the
   wind blowing through the
   trees. He pulled the blanket
   over his head and wished the
   storm would end.
   Brian was very

   _____ .

3. Nan looked at the clock. It was
   not lunch time. She wished she
   had eaten breakfast. She would
   be very glad when it was time
   to go to the cafeteria.
   Nan felt

   _____ .

4. The firefighter climbed the
   ladder. He helped the child
   come down the ladder. Then
   he went back up to help
   someone else.
   The firefighter is

   _____ .

5. The insect sat on Karen's
   fingernail. It had six legs. It had
   a black body. She wished she
   had a magnifying glass to look
   at it more closely.
   The insect is

   _____ .

Brainwork! Write a noun to go with each word in the word box. Example:
tiny (kitten)

14   FS-32028 Critical Thinking

Name _____

Read each story. Write a sentence to answer each question.

1. The dog ran inside the doghouse. He barked when he heard the thunder. He yelped when he saw the lightning in the sky. He curled up in the back corner of the doghouse.

   How was the dog feeling?

   _____

   _____

2. Kate looked at her watch. She grabbed her sweater and her books. She hurried out the door. She ran to the corner where the school bus stopped.

   What time of day was it?

   _____

   _____

3. Brent raised his hand. He showed the broken pencil point to the teacher. She told Brent that he could get up from his seat. He walked across the room. He took his pencil with him.

   Why did Brent raise his hand?

   _____

   _____

4. Mother fed the baby. Then she put the baby in her crib. She covered the baby with a blanket. She closed the curtains. Then she quietly walked out of the room.

   Why did mother need to close the curtains?

   _____

   _____

Brainwork! Draw a picture of a girl playing in the snow. Write five sentences to describe your picture.

Name _____

Read the story. Follow the directions below each story. Do your BEST!!

1. "Mark, let's wash your finger and put on a bandage. Then you can go outside and play again."

   Circle the clue word that tells you Mark hurt his finger.
   Underline the words that tell you Mark is not badly hurt.

2. Daddy said, "Whoops! We are out of film." Then he put a new roll inside the camera. He turned the knob so it was ready to use.

   Circle the clue word that lets you know someone will probably take a photograph.
   Underline the phrase that lets you know the old film was used up.

3. "Look, Mother. It burned the bread again," said Mike. "This time instead of having it fixed, I'll buy a new toaster," said Mother.

   Circle the words that let you know that the toaster is not working right.
   Underline the phrase that lets you know Mother does not want to get it repaired.

4. Nan took off the lid and dumped the pieces on the table. Then she started to fit the pieces together to make a picture.

   Circle the word that tells you the pieces were not in a paper bag.
   Underline the phrase that lets you know she is working on a puzzle.

Brainwork! Draw a picture that shows what Mark was doing before he got hurt.

How Did They Know?

In the stories below, Dad and Mom each seem to know something without being told. How do they know? Read each story carefully. Think about the answer choices. On the lines, write the sentence that tells how they know.

Power Out!

Mom came home from work late one night. Everyone was asleep. When she tried to turn on the living room light, nothing happened. Then she tried the kitchen light. Finally, she lit a candle and looked at the clock. "The power must have gone out at 10:43," she said.

Mom knew exactly what time the power went off. How did she know?

- She came home after 10:43.
- The kitchen light didn't work.
- The clock had stopped at 10:43.

1. _____

Long Gone?

Dad looked around the kitchen. He spied some cookie crumbs on a napkin and on the counter a glass of ice with a few drops of lemonade left in it. There was a note on the table that said, "I am going to Manny's for a couple of hours. Love, Nick."

Dad knew Nick hadn't been gone long. How did he know?

- The note said what time he left.
- The ice in the glass hadn't melted.
- Nick had eaten a cookie.

2. _____

Try This! Nick went to Manny's. Write three things you think *Manny's* could mean.

Read the clues. Write the answer on the line.

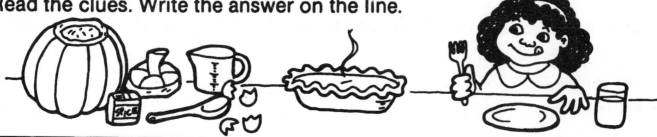

1. I can learn to do tricks.
   I have colorful feathers.
   I can learn to talk.
   What am I?

   _____

   a puppet, a parrot, a puppy

2. I am in the sky.
   I have many bands of color.
   You see me after it rains.
   What am I?

   _____

   the sun, a cloud, a rainbow

3. Use me to make a pie or
   carve a face on me.
   Roast and eat my seeds.
   What am I?

   _____

   an apple, a pumpkin, a cherry

4. I list words in ABC order.
   I can help you find out what a
   word means.
   What am I?

   _____

   a dictionary, a storybook,
   a magazine

5. I have letters and numbers.
   I have a bell.
   Use me to talk to people.
   What am I?

   _____

   a letter, a telephone,
   a post card

6. You can read me everyday.
   I tell about the weather
   and what just happened.
   What am I?

   _____

   a book, a story, a newspaper

Brainwork! Write clues about a person. Ask a friend to guess who it is.

Read the story. Follow the directions below each story. **You can do it!**

1. She put on her costume and mask. "My princess costume is beautiful. I'm so glad my mother knows how to sew," Ann said.

   Circle the word that tells you that Ann's mother probably made her costume.
   Underline the words that make you think she is going to a Halloween party.

2. Rick led the horse out of the barn. He put the saddle on the horse. He remembered looking at the colt when it was born. Now it was big and strong. Neigh-h-h-h !

   Circle the word that makes you think Rick will ride the horse.
   Underline the words that let you know Rick saw the colt when it was not big and strong.

3. Jay used the shovel to dig. The soil got soft. Then he opened the package of seeds. "Mother loves the way these taste, so I hope these grow," Jay thought.

   Circle the word that tells you Jay is planting something you can eat.
   Underline the words that tell you the soil was hard.

4. The teacher asked a student to close the curtains. He asked another student to turn off the lights. The room got quiet. He turned on the projector.

   Circle the word that tells you they are going to see a film.
   Underline the words that tell you the room had been noisy.

Brainwork! Draw four kinds of plants Jay might be planting.

Name _____

Read the story. Read the two sentences after the story.
Write the **true** sentence on the line.

1. Sam crossed his fingers. Then he opened his mouth. The dentist
   looked at Sam's teeth. He told Sam he was doing a good job caring
   for his teeth.

   a. Sam has too many cavities.
   b. Sam has no cavities.

   _____

2. There were leaves all over the ground. Amy helped her mother rake
   the leaves into big piles. Amy took the lid off the big trash can.

   a. They put the leaves in the can.
   b. They spread the leaves across the grass.

   _____

3. Daddy filled the tub with warm water. He opened the bottle of
   special shampoo. Then he picked up the dog and put him in the
   water.

   a. The dog is learning to swim.
   b. The dog is getting a bath.

   _____

4. Joe spread the icing on the cake. He put eight candles on the top.
   Then he told everyone to look at the fancy cake.

   a. It is someone's birthday.
   b. Dinner is ready now.

   _____

Brainwork! Draw a picture of the cake Joe might make next year.

         FS-32028 Critical Thinking

Name _____

Read the story. Write a word from the
Word Box to complete each sentence.

Word Box

surprised   windy

cranky   farm

proud

1. Sam fed the chickens. Then he
let the cows out of the barn.
After school he would take a
ride on his horse.
Sam lives on a

_____

2. Pat hurried home from school.
He pulled the paper out of his
folder. He wanted to show
Mother the big gold star on his
spelling test.
Pat is

_____ of himself.

3. "This is the kind of day I have
been waiting for," said Amy. "It
is just perfect for my new kite.
This is the biggest kite I have
ever flown."
It is a

_____ day.

4. "Wow! This is great!" said Mike.
"Even though it is my birthday,
I didn't know there would be a
party!"
Mike is

_____

5. The baby didn't want to eat. He
cried when his mother picked
him up. Then he cried when
she put him down. His mother
said she didn't know what was
wrong.
The baby is

_____

Brainwork! Draw three faces to illustrate the three words that describe
feelings in the Word Box. Write the word under each face.

     21   FS-32028 Critical Thinking

Read Between the Lines

If you read carefully, you can often learn information that is not actually stated. For example, if you read that Maria brought home her report card, you would know that Maria goes to school.

Read each story below. Circle **yes** or **no** after each statement.

1. Marci and Tom are twins. They are each on a soccer team. Marci's team has won one more game than Tom's team.

   a. Marci and Tom are on the same team.   yes   no
   b. Marci and Tom have the same mother.   yes   no

2. Daryl and Les are going to Cub Scout camp 20 miles from their school. Daryl's sister will drive them there.

   a. Daryl's sister is younger than Daryl.   yes   no
   b. Daryl and Les are boys.   yes   no

3. Carl is happy that his birthday is on Halloween. Ten months ago, on his seventh birthday, he had a big trick-or-treat party.

   a. Carl's birthday is on October 31.   yes   no
   b. Carl will turn eight on his next birthday.   yes   no

4. Jean has only two cousins. Both are sons of her Uncle Will and his wife Anne. Uncle Will is Jean's mother's brother.

   a. Jean's cousins are boys.   yes   no
   b. Will and Anne have no daughters.   yes   no

Try This! Dianne and Betsy have the same mother and father. Dianne's birthday is March 18. Betsy is exactly one year younger than Dianne. Write two more things you know about them.

FS-32028 Critical Thinking

Read each story. Write a sentence that answers each question.

1. Grandpa picked up the sewing box. He found a needle and thread. Then he picked up the shirt and the button.

   Why did Grandpa need a needle, thread and a button?

   _____

   _____

2. Amy opened the cupboard. She got out the bag of food. Then she put the food in the dish and called the puppy.

   How can you tell that the puppy knows his name?

   _____

   _____

3. The babysitter asked the twins to sit beside her. She opened the book. Then she told the twins she wanted them to take turns turning the pages. She told them she wanted them to listen.

   How do you know that the twins are not babies?

   _____

   _____

4. The children could see the smoke from the locomotive. The train was coming closer and closer. When the train got very close, they covered their ears.

   Why did the children cover their ears?

   _____

   _____

Brainwork! Would you like to be a twin? Why or why not?

Read Between the Lines

Read each story carefully. Then follow the directions below it.

Marie Helps Herself

When Marie stepped off the yellow bus, she noticed a rip in her bookbag. Knowing that Mom was getting ready to leave for her evening class, Marie got the needle and thread from the box herself.

1. Underline the words in the story that let you know that Marie will sew the rip. Circle the words that let you know that Marie was returning home from school.
2. Why do you think Marie did not ask Mom to fix her bookbag?

   _____

3. How do you know that Marie has probably sewed before?

   _____

Gene Loves Books

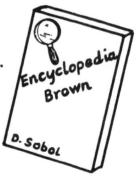

Gene sat down to read after dinner as he always does. When he opened the book for the first time, he noticed some scribbling on one of the pages. Gene loves books and was angry that someone who had borrowed the book before him hadn't taken care of it.

4. Underline the words in the story that let you know that Gene takes good care of books. Circle the words that let you know that Gene usually reads after dinner.
5. How do you know that the book is probably a library book?_____

   _____

6. Why didn't Gene notice the scribbling before?_____

   _____

Try This! Which of these two people seems more like you? Write why.

24   FS-32028 Critical Thinking

Name _____

Read the clues. Write the answer on the line.

1. I grow underground.
    You can eat me cooked or raw.
    I am orange with green leaves
    on top.
    What am I?

    _____

    an orange, a carrot, a radish

2. I can be in a tree.
    I am made of twigs and string.
    I am used in the spring.
    What am I?

    _____

    a nest, a branch, a bird

3. I am at school.
    I keep books inside me.
    You can lean on me when you
    write.
    What am I?

    _____

    a desk, a pencil, a classroom

4. I am white or brown.
    I will break if you drop me.
    You can break me and eat me.
    What am I?

    _____

    a dish, an egg, breakfast

5. I have two hands.
    I have numbers.
    I will tell you when to go to
    bed.
    What am I?

    _____

    a puppy, a teacher, a clock

6. I have three colors.
    Each color lights up.
    I help people know when to
    stop and go.
    What am I?

    _____

    a flag, a stop sign, a traffic light

Brainwork! Write clues about a vegetable. Ask a friend to guess what it is.

Name _____

THINK!

Read each story. Write a sentence that answers each question.

1. Mike saw some shiny objects on the floor. He picked them up. They were two quarters and one dime. He gave the money to his teacher. He told her where he found them.

   What kind of a person is Mike?

   _____

   _____

2. Sara felt tired. She did not want to get out of bed. She did not want to play or eat. She didn't want to watch her favorite show on television.

   What could be wrong with Sara?

   _____

   _____

3. Dan looked at the puppies. He picked up the brown one. Then he held the black one. Dan could not decide which puppy he liked best.

   How was Dan feeling?

   _____

   _____

4. The teacher said, "You have all turned in your homework this week. You have earned an extra play period."

   Who is the teacher talking to?

   Keep up the good work!

   _____

   _____

Brainwork! Draw a picture showing where Dan was as he looked at the puppies.

26   FS-32028 Critical Thinking

Name

Bobby's Ride

Read the story about Bobby. Follow the directions below each part.

Part A

Bobby came in his front door with a tear in his jeans and a scrape on his knee. He told his mom, "While I was riding out front, a baby bird landed on the bike path in front of me. I swerved to keep from hitting it."

1. Underline the words that let you know Bobby was not riding in the street. Circle the words in the story that tell you he was riding near home.
2. What clue in the story lets you know that Bobby fell?

_____

3. Based on the story, how do you think Bobby feels about animals?

Part B

As Bobby was washing his scrape, there was a knock at the door. When he opened it, Jenny said, "Don't worry, Bobby. When you left, I picked your bike up off the ground and saw the bird safe in the tree."

4. Underline the words in the story that let you know that Bobby left his bike lying on the path. Circle the words that let you know that Jenny knew why Bobby swerved.
5. How can you tell that Jenny was near Bobby when the accident happened? _____
6. How can you tell that Bobby rushed right home after he fell?

_____

Try This! Based on the story, describe the kind of friend Jenny is.

27

Name _____

Read the story. Write the answers to the questions.

Camp Sky High

Matt and Jay were in their bedroom packing for camp. "Be sure to bring your swim suit and fishing pole," Matt said.

"I have my fishing pole all set to go. I hope to win the big fishing contest again this year," said Jay.

Matt put his warm jacket into the suitcase. He wanted to wear it at night around the campfire. "I'm glad we can stay for two weeks this year. One week goes too fast! We are going to have a great time!"

1. Jay and Matt are probably brothers because _____

   _____ .

2. You can tell Matt expects the nights to be cool because _____

   _____ .

3. What clue word tells you Jay has been to Camp Sky High before? _____ .

4. How can you tell that the boys wanted to stay longer last year? _____

   _____

5. Camp Sky High is probably located in the
   (city, desert, mountains) _____ .

6. When the boys arrive at camp, they will probably be feeling
   (homesick, happy, angry) _____ .

Brainwork! Pretend you are at Camp Sky High. Write a note from camp to your family.

Name _____

Read the story. Write the answers to the questions.

Very Special Visitors

For a birthday treat, Dan's mother was taking him to the zoo. He could invite a friend to go, too. "The newspaper says that they will only be there for one more month," Mother said.

"I have always wanted to see real pandas. They look so cute in pictures. I hope they are as much fun to watch as the monkeys," said Danny. "I know Chris will like the zoo because he reads books about animals."

1. You can tell there is a newspaper article about pandas

   in the zoo because _____.

2. How do you think Chris feels about animals? _____

   _____.

3. How can you tell Danny has been to a zoo before? _____

   _____.

4. Danny probably knows what pandas look like because _____

   _____.

5. How can you tell the pandas are not always at the zoo? _____

   _____.

6. Chris is Danny's (brother, cousin, friend) _____

Brainwork! Choose an animal you think is cute. Write five words to describe it.

Snowball's Escape

Jason got the hamster food from the shelf and walked toward Snowball's cage. But Snowball was not in sight. He was not on his running wheel or asleep under his bedding. There was nowhere else in the cage Snowball could be hiding!

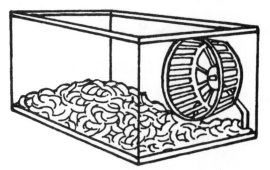

At first Jason wondered how Snowball could have escaped. Then he realized that the cage cover was leaning against his bed. Jason felt guilty since he was the only one who took care of Snowball.

Suddenly Jason heard a sound from inside the closet next to the cage. When he opened the door, there was Snowball curled up in Jason's sneaker!

1. What kind of animal is Snowball?_____ How do you know?

_____

2. Is Snowball male or female? _____How do you know?

_____

3. How was Snowball able to escape? _____

4. Why did Jason feel guilty? _____

_____

5. In what room was Snowball's cage? _____

   How do you know? _____

Try This! Write why you think Snowball crawled into Jason's sneaker.

Circle the right answers for each question.

1. What do you do in math?

   add   divide   swim   multiply   subtract

2. Which jewels could be used to make a ring?

   ruby   jade   diamond   emerald   apple

3. Which ones are snakes?

   cobra   hawk   boa   garter   copperhead

4. Which ones are baby animals?

   dog   colt   cub   calf   kitten

5. Which ones are planets?

   Mars   Venus   Jupiter   Texas   Earth

6. Which ones are made of water?

   ocean   ice   puddle   stream   hill

7. Which ones give off light?

   sun   desk   fire   lamp   torch

8. What would you find on a kitchen table?

   salt   plate   barn   knife   napkin

9. Which ones tell how something feels?

   hard   sharp   lemon   sticky   soft

10. Which ones are round?

   ball   donut   penny   box   bubble

11. Which ones have two legs?

   chicken   person   bird   duck   cow

12. What would you see in a garden?

   desk   corn   scarecrow   hoe   carrots

31   FS-32028 Critical Thinking

Write each word from the word box under the right category.

1. Sounds	2. U.S. States	3. Body Parts

Word Box

skin	hoot	Texas	laugh	bones	Hawaii	muscles
fizz	ribs	lungs	Maine	blood	squeak	whisper
Ohio	howl	growl	heart	Kansas	Alaska	New York

Name _____   Skill: Categorization

Mind Teasers

Write what each group
of words has in common.

1. piggy bank   purse   savings   cash register

_____

2. bench   stool   sofa   chair

_____

3. nurse   milkman   doctor   maid

_____

4. read   blink   stare   cross

_____

5. penguin   zebra   panda bear   newspaper

_____

6. hiss   giggle   snore   creak

_____

7. Eskimo   igloo   polar bear   icebergs

_____

8. stable   saddle   harness   gallop

_____

9. Red Rover   Handball   Tag   Dodgeball

_____

10. coat   blanket   fire   mittens

_____

Name _____

Write the name of the category at the **top** of each box.
Then write two more things that belong to each category.

1.	2.
bottle crib diaper _____ _____	Dad sister Mom _____ _____

3.	4.	5.
cake lake bake _____ _____	pine maple oak _____ _____	tires brake engine _____ _____

6.	7.	8.
bacon cereal eggs _____ _____	heater iron coffee pot _____ _____	igloo castle apartment _____ _____

Write a word for each category that
starts with the letter given.

	Animals	Transportation	Jobs
T			
S			
C			
A			

	Names of Girls	Sports	Food
B			
S			
H			
T			

Write each word from the word box under the right category.

1. Feelings	2. Sports	3. Materials

Word Box

sick	golf	steel	brass	boxing	excited	swimming
wood	cloth	glass	brave	tennis	hockey	baseball
sad	angry	happy	scared	rubber	plastic	football

Circle the right answers for each question.

1. Which ones are jobs?

   nurse   barber   pilot   carpenter   puppy

2. Which ones are parts of a house?

   grass   door   window   wall   roof

3. What would you find in a forest?

   trees   whale   chipmunk   pine cones   deer

4. Which ones are time words?

   day   year   penny   month   week

5. Which ones are trees?

   pine   elm   oak   daisy   spruce

6. Which ones live in the ocean?

   seal   pig   shark   octopus   whale

7. Which ones are countries?

   Japan   U.S.A.   Canada   Kansas   Mexico

8. Which ones are directions?

   far   north   east   south   west

9. In which ones could you ride?

   car   truck   wagon   boat   stove

10. Which ones are too heavy to carry?

   elephant   feather   house   car   cow

11. Which ones can you wear?

   pants   coat   shirt   lamp   shoes

12. Which ones measure something?

   ruler   teaspoon   purse   cup   yardstick

Write the name of the category at the **top** of each box.
Then write two more things that belong to each category.

1.	2.
daisy rose violet _____ _____	fingers head feet _____ _____

3.	4.	5.
farm zoo desert _____ _____	snow dew tornado _____ _____	Canada England France _____ _____

6.	7.	8.
dentist teacher grocer _____ _____	minute week year _____ _____	sink soap toothpaste _____ _____

FS-32028 Critical Thinking

Name _____

Write the name of the holiday for each picture.
The answers are in the pot of gold.

1. _____

Pot of Gold

Washington's Birthday
Columbus Day
Fourth of July
Flag Day
Thanksgiving
Lincoln's Birthday
Easter
Halloween
New Year
April Fools' Day

2. _____

3. _____

4. _____

5. _____

6. _____

7. _____

8. _____

9. _____

10. _____

FS-32028 Critical Thinking

Mind Teasers

Write what each group
of words has in common.

1. horseshoe   four-leaf clover   number seven

_____

2. window   mirror   vase   crystal ball

_____

3. rabbit   marshmallow   pillow   cotton

_____

4. whizz   quiz   Liz   fizz

_____

5. sled   snowshoes   skis   toboggan

_____

6. sailboat   kite   windmill   pinwheel

_____

7. unicorn   dragon   troll   leprechaun

_____

8. math   reading   science   music

_____

9. bitter   sweet   sour   salty

_____

10. runway   airplane   control tower   tickets

_____

FS-32028 Critical Thinking

Write the name of the category at the **top** of each box.
Then write two more things that belong to each category.

1.	2.	3.
white rye whole wheat _____ _____	surfing ice skating basketball _____ _____	sailboat raft canoe _____ _____
4.	5.	6.
Maryland Alabama Kentucky _____ _____	apples oranges plums _____ _____	Saturn Neptune Pluto _____ _____
7.	8.	
piano violin flute _____ _____	poodle cocker spaniel collie _____ _____	

Write each word from the word box under the right category.

1. Classroom	2. Birthday Things	3. Musical Instruments

Word Box

cake	drums	desks	piano	suckers	cymbals	scissors
harp	candy	gifts	paints	erasers	paper	nut cups
tuba	chalk	flute	guitar	pencils	candles	ice cream

FS-32028 Critical Thinking

Mind Teasers

Write what each group
of words has in common.

1. hat   bonnet   hood   cap

_____

2. clouds   bird   airplane   sun

_____

3. Clean up your room.   Put on your jacket.   Be careful.

_____

4. lamp   flashlight   lighthouse   firefly

_____

5. wheat   white   rye   sourdough

_____

6. Brontosaurus   Tyrannosaurus Rex   Stegosaurus

_____

7. Friday the 13th   breaking a mirror   walking under a ladder

_____

8. donut   bead   swiss cheese   tire

_____

9. kangaroo   frog   rabbit   grasshopper

_____

10. march   tiptoe   jump   stamp

_____

43   FS-32028 Critical Thinking

Name _____

Circle the right answers for each question.

1. Which ones are birds?

monkey   crow   owl   parrot   dove

2. Which ones are easy to lift?

pillow   car   pencil   spoon   comb

3. What would you need to go camping?

tent   sleeping bag   cat   flashlight   compass

4. What would you find in a living room?

TV   couch   table   bathtub   lamp

5. Which ones are your relatives?

uncle   grandpa   aunt   cousin   teacher

6. Which sports do not need a ball?

hockey   ping pong   skating   diving   skiing

7. What could you use in the rain?

trunks   umbrella   boots   coat   hood

8. Which ones are tools?

saw   shovel   ax   hammer   pants

9. Which ones are made out of cloth?

dress   curtains   shirt   stove   bedspread

10. Who works at a school?

florist   principal   teacher   custodian   secretary

11. Which ones can be found in the air?

helicopter   jet   train   blimp   glider

12. Which ones are names for boys?

Adam   Scott   Mark   Brad   Holly

44

Name _____ **Categorization**

Write the letter that names the category for each group of words.

a. Jobs	f. Clothes	k. Winter Sports
b. Homes	g. Lincoln	l. Start with "P"
c. States	h. Fat Things	m. Rhyming Words
d. Trees	i. Round Things	n. Can Hold Liquids
e. Sounds	j. Jewelry	o. Things That Cut

1. log cabin — Abe — lawyer — 16th — ____

2. skiing — ice skating — sledding — hockey — ____

3. gumball — wheel — circle — peas — ____

4. model — carpenter — nurse — teacher — ____

5. California — Oklahoma — Delaware — Texas — ____

6. cottage — tepee — mansion — cabin — ____

7. chime — gulp — whine — howl — ____

8. coat — shirt — pants — socks — ____

9. Humpty-Dumpty — pig — hippo — cushion — ____

10. cake — lake — rake — snake — ____

11. walnut — willow — redwood — oak — ____

12. ring — necklace — bracelet — earrings — ____

13. cup — mug — glass — jug — ____

14. lawn mower — ax — scissors — knife — ____

15. puppy — puddle — plant — person — ____

Name _____

Write who or what goes with each story. The storybook will help you!

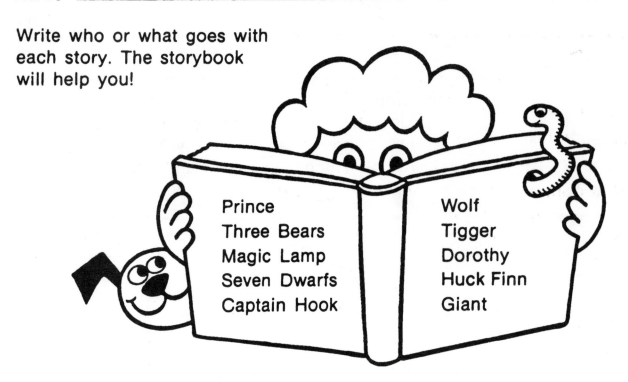

Prince
Three Bears
Magic Lamp
Seven Dwarfs
Captain Hook

Wolf
Tigger
Dorothy
Huck Finn
Giant

1. Goldilocks _____

2. Cinderella _____

3. Peter Pan _____

4. Three Little Pigs _____

5. Jack and the Beanstalk _____

6. Wizard of Oz _____

7. Winnie-the-Pooh _____

8. Tom Sawyer _____

9. Aladdin _____

10. Snow White _____

 FS-32028 Critical Thinking

As It Is

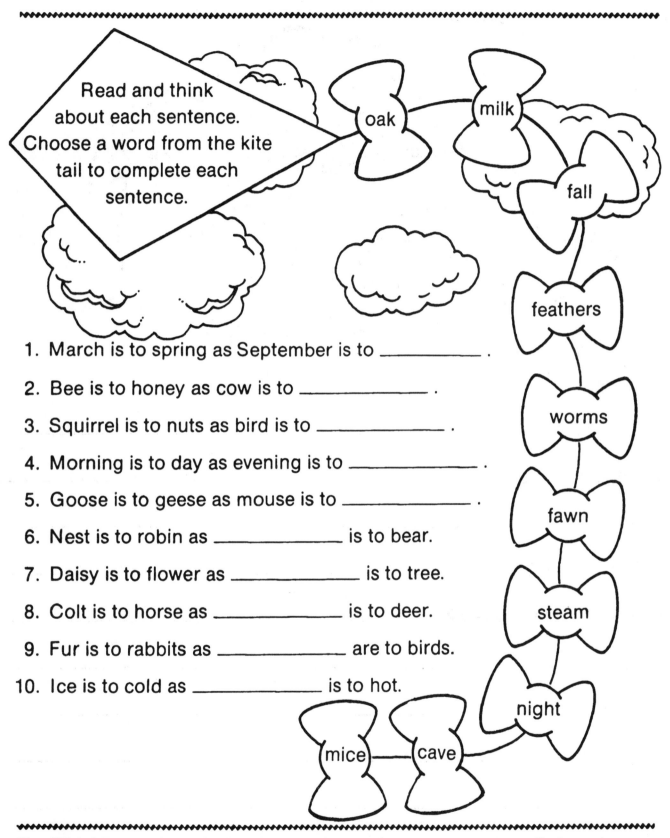

Read and think about each sentence. Choose a word from the kite tail to complete each sentence.

oak

milk

fall

feathers

worms

fawn

steam

night

mice

cave

1. March is to spring as September is to _____ .

2. Bee is to honey as cow is to _____ .

3. Squirrel is to nuts as bird is to _____ .

4. Morning is to day as evening is to _____ .

5. Goose is to geese as mouse is to _____ .

6. Nest is to robin as _____ is to bear.

7. Daisy is to flower as _____ is to tree.

8. Colt is to horse as _____ is to deer.

9. Fur is to rabbits as _____ are to birds.

10. Ice is to cold as _____ is to hot.

Try This! Pairs of words that go together in the same way are called *analogies*. Create three analogies.

47

FS-32028 Critical Thinking

Each pair of words goes together in the same way.
What is the relationship? Write each one on the line.

1. Baseball   is to mitt   as
   boxing   is to gloves.

   _____

   _____

2. Goat   is to kid   as
   lion   is to cub.

   _____

   _____

3. TV   is to living room as
   stove   is to kitchen.

   _____

   _____

4. Snow   is to white   as
   stop sign is to red.

   _____

   _____

5. Flea   is to jumping   as
   sea gull   is to flying.

   _____

   _____

6. Boy   is to man   as
   girl   is to woman.

   _____

   _____

7. Fox   is to ax   as
   quiz   is to fuzz.

   _____

   _____

8. Christmas is to December as
   Thanksgiving is to November.

   _____

   _____

Each pair of words goes together in the same way.
Write the missing word on the line. The word box will help you.

1. Ant is to insect as robin is to _____ .

2. Monday is to Tuesday as January is to _____ .

3. Circle is to ball as square is to _____ .

4. Barber is to hair as mail carrier is to _____ .

5. Octopus is to eight as duck is to _____ .

6. Hammer is to tool box as shirt is to _____ .

7. Drum is to tuba as apple is to _____ .

8. Bee is to sting as dog is to _____ .

9. Halloween is to pumpkin as Easter is to _____ .

10. Hand is to arm as foot is to _____ .

Word Box			
letters	two	box	trumpet
bird	leg	bite	egg
November	February	banana	closet

Each pair of words goes together in the same way.
Write the missing word on the line. The word box will help you.

1. Tiger is to jungle as pig is to _____ .

2. Tent is to sleeping bag as house is to _____ .

3. State is to New York as country is to _____ .

4. Water is to boat as land is to _____ .

5. Carpenter is to hammer as gardener is to _____ .

6. Swim is to water as fly is to _____ .

7. Dog is to bark as duck is to _____ .

8. Touch is to fur as taste is to _____ .

9. Lincoln is to sixteenth as Washington is to _____ .

10. Pillow is to soft as rock is to _____ .

Word Box			
bed	France	hoe	hard
quack	farm	moo	first
pizza	air	water	train

Each pair of words goes together in the same way.
Write the missing word on the line. The word box will help you.

1. Roar is to lion as meow is to _____ .

2. Crow is to hawk as rose is to _____ .

3. Bee is to honey as cow is to _____ .

4. Car is to land as helicopter is to _____ .

5. Tar is to black as sky is to _____ .

6. Fawn is to deer as calf is to _____ .

7. Teacher is to school as doctor is to _____ .

8. Jockey is to horse as surfer is to _____ .

9. Fingers are to ten as ears are to _____ .

10. Dry is to wet as hot is to _____ .

Word Box			
cow	hospital	daisy	warm
cat	board	air	milk
two	red	blue	cold

Read the words in each box. Write a cause from the Word Box.

1.
spent money
have packages
_____

2.
stay in bed
fever
_____

Word Box
traffic light
autumn
fan
rain
illness
summer
shopping
scary movie

3.
cars stopped
people walked
_____

4.
colored leaves
squirrels gather nuts
_____

5.
air moves
cooler
_____

6.
frightened
have nightmares
_____

7.
hot days
daylight after dinner
_____

8.
wet road
need umbrellas
_____

Just for Fun! Write an answer to the question.
Why is the little dog wagging its tail?

FS-32028 Critical Thinking

Read the words in each box. Write a cause from the Word Box.

1. turn on water pick up soap _____	2. get a pencil take out paper _____	**Word Box** circus vacation write game crying school wash hands bake
3. tent parade _____	4. tears frown _____	
5. mix batter pans in oven _____	6. pack suitcase say goodbye _____	
7. take turns roll the dice _____	8. take books take lunch _____	

FLOUR
x x x x

OIL

Just for Fun! Write to show what happened next.
The skateboard went faster and faster!

Read the words in each box. Write a cause from the Word Box.

1. put on bathing suit jump in water _____	2. put on coat open the door _____
3. pick up receiver say hello _____	4. get crayons get art paper _____
5. get a needle use some thread _____	6. look to right look to left _____
7. lick a stamp seal the envelope _____	8. say "ouch" finger bleeds _____

Word Box

want to sew   a cut
will cross a road   want to draw
will go out   telephone rang
want to swim   will mail a card

Just for Fun! Write to tell what happened next.
The wind blew the umbrella out of her hand.

     54   FS-32028 Critical Thinking

Read the words in each box. Write a cause from the Word Box.

Word Box
winter
locked
fire
hole in pocket
wind
puppy
birthday
night

1.
flames
smoke

_____

2.
lost key
lost coins

_____

3.
blowing leaves
kites can fly

_____

4.
cold weather
gets dark early

_____

5.
barking
chewed shoe

_____

6.
need a key
will not open

_____

7.
dark
bedtime

_____

8.
cake
candles

_____

WOW!

Just for Fun! Write to tell the reason this happened.
That horse is wearing red socks.

Name ______________________________ Skill: Determining the cause

Read the words in each box. Write a cause from the Word Box.

1. puddles wet streets ________	2. dream rest ________
3. cool days leaves fall ________	4. flowers bloom birds build nests ________
5. tired out of breath ________	6. wake up get dressed ________
7. chew swallow ________	8. no school time to play ________

Word Box
sleep
eat
weekend
rain
morning
running
autumn
spring

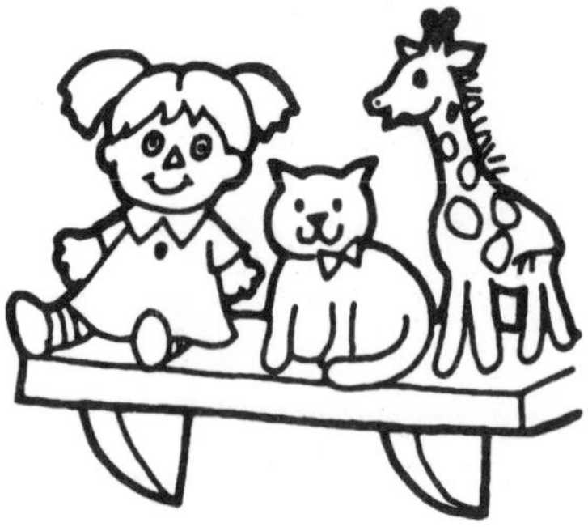

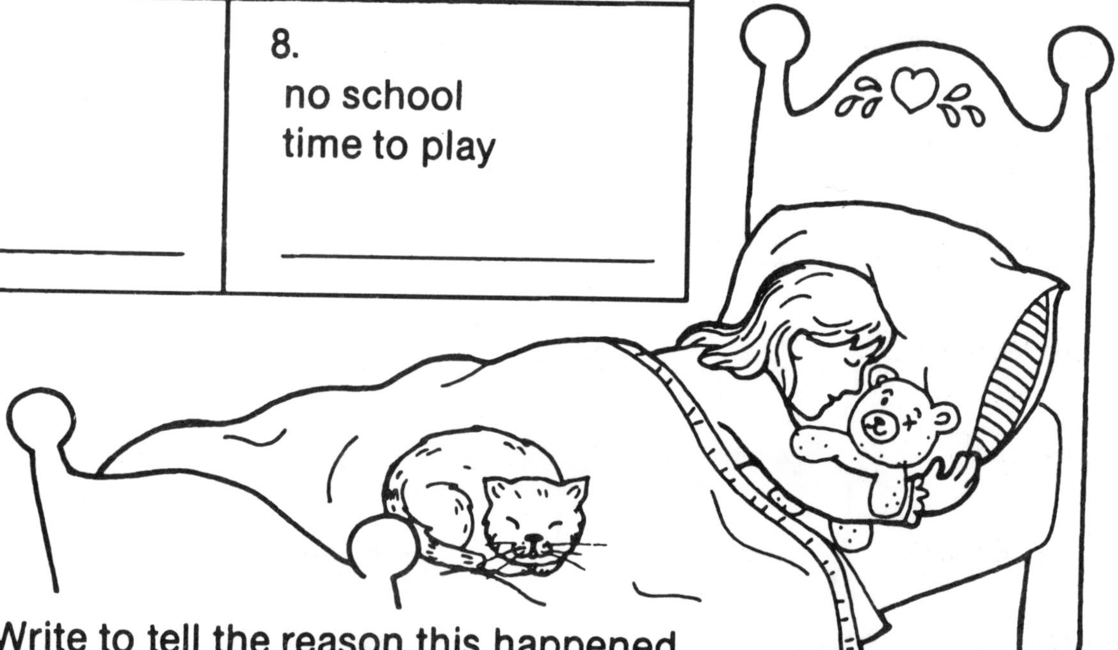

Just for Fun! Write to tell the reason this happened.
The boy's picture was in the newspaper.

Write a word from the Word Box to complete each sentence.

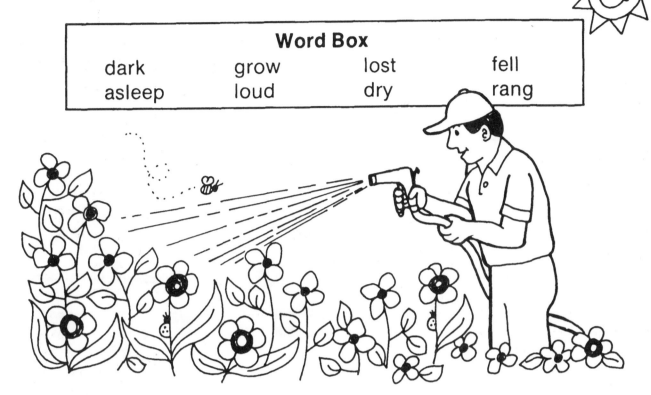

Word Box			
dark	grow	lost	fell
asleep	loud	dry	rang

1. Dad watered the plants because they were _____ .

2. Grandmother was tired, so she fell _____ .

3. Mother opened the door because the doorbell _____ .

4. Brent is locked out because he _____ his key.

5. The glass broke when it _____ to the floor.

6. Sue watered the tree to make it _____ .

7. It is hard to see because it is _____ .

8. Turn down the radio because it is _____ .

Just for Fun! Write to tell why.
Why is the cup broken?

Write a phrase from the Word Box to complete each sentence.

Word Box

cars would stop   would not tip
train was coming   gathered twigs
would see her   heard the sirens
she was cold   caught a fish

1. The cars pulled over when they _____.

2. The birds were building nests so they _____.

3. I sat down in the boat so it _____.

4. The lady shivered because _____.

5. The policeman held out his arm so the _____.

6. The gates came down because the _____.

7. The fishing line pulled tight when I _____.

8. Mother waved so I _____.

Just for Fun! Write to tell what happened next.
Dad dropped the big bag of groceries!

       58

Write a word from the Word Box to complete each sentence.

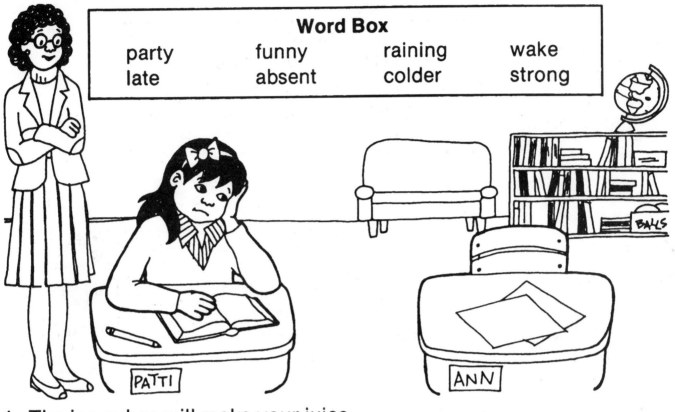

Word Box

| party | funny | raining | wake |
| late | absent | colder | strong |

1. The ice cubes will make your juice _____ .

2. The teacher laughed because the joke was _____ .

3. Dad will pick up the big box because he is _____ .

4. Patti feels lonely because her friend is _____ .

5. The traffic jam made us _____ for school.

6. The thunderstorm made me _____ up during the night.

7. My friend is excited because the _____ is today.

8. She needs her raincoat because it is _____ .

Just for Fun! Write to show why this happened.
Why is that puppy's nose purple?

Skill: Determining cause and effect

Write a phrase from the Word Box to complete each sentence.

Word Box

is a collector	it is wet
would look pretty	would stay out
know the number	bug bit her
would be straight	be safe

1. Mother closed the screen so bugs _____ .

2. Meg scratched her arm because a _____ .

3. Dan saves stamps because he _____ .

4. The match won't light because _____ .

5. The teacher used a ruler so the line _____ .

6. I used the telephone book because I didn't _____ .

7. Kate wrapped the gift so it _____ .

8. He locked the gate so the puppy would _____ .

Just for Fun! Write to tell what happened next.
She put two new batteries in the flashlight.

Name _____

Circle the correct word.
Then write the word on the line
to complete each sentence.

1. The cake burned because the oven was too _____.

   new   hot   big

2. We can make a snowman because it _____.

   rained   hailed   snowed

3. The baby was asleep, so I _____.

   whispered   screamed   shouted

4. She hid because she was _____.

   scared   hungry   old

5. The dog is wagging her tail because she is _____.

   angry   shy   friendly

6. It is cold because the window is _____.

   closed   open   new

7. She covered her ears because the music was _____.

   beautiful   loud   soft

8. We washed our hands, so they were _____.

   soft   clean   dirty

9. I stayed up too late, so I feel _____.

   silly   strong   tired

10. My alarm clock didn't ring, so I was _____.

   awake   late   early

Just for Fun! Write to tell what happened next.
He jumped out of the tree!

61   FS-32028 Critical Thinking

Name _____

Circle the correct word.
Then write the word on the line
to complete each sentence.

1. When I heard the riddle, I _____ .
              cried   laughed   frowned

2. When the balloon popped, I _____ .
             danced   sang   jumped

3. I have no cavities, so I am _____ .
             sad   happy   worried

4. I slipped because the sidewalk was _____ .
             icy   warm   flat

5. We are going on a trip, so we need to _____ .
             crawl   pack   fight

6. I need a drink of water because I am _____ .
             thirsty   hungry   happy

7. She shared her toys because she is _____ .
             mean   tall   nice

8. Daddy can reach the shelf because he is _____ .
             old   fat   tall

9. We play together because we are _____ .
             funny   friends   smart

10. Don't play in the street because it is _____ .
             dry   dangerous   wide

Just for Fun! Write to tell the reason this happened.
Kim was late for school.

                      FS-32028 Critical Thinking

Name _____ Skill: **Determining cause and effect**

Write a word from the Word Box to complete each sentence.

Word Box

empty	wind	tight	hot
sugar	dirty	sneeze	save

Try again, Pedro!

1. Wash your hands because they are _____ .

2. The pie is too sweet because it contains too much _____ .

3. My cold is making me _____ a lot.

4. The button popped off because my jacket is too _____ .

5. The leaves blew off the tree because of the _____ .

6. Turn off the lights so we can _____ energy.

7. The cookies burned because the oven was too _____ .

8. Mother drove far so the gas tank was almost _____ .

Just for Fun! Write to tell what happened next.
The cat put its paw in the green paint.

Name _____

Write a phrase from the Word Box to complete each sentence.

Word Box

ride her bike	has a leak
took the picture	touch the wall
hands were cold	it is dull
hungry before lunch	a new one

Sure I'll have more juice, Mom!

1. My shoelace broke, so I need _____ .

2. I put on my gloves because my _____ .

3. The paint is wet, so do not _____ .

4. She has training wheels because she can't _____ .

5. Eat breakfast so you are not _____ .

6. The knife won't cut because _____ .

7. My bike tire is soft because it _____ .

8. The camera clicked when I _____ .

Just for Fun! Write to tell why this happened.
The girl yelled, "Hooray, I found it first!"

Circle the correct word.
Then write the word on the line to complete each sentence.

1. I can't play because I am _____.

    happy   ill   wise

2. There is no school because it is _____.

    sunny   cloudy   Sunday

3. When the scary ghost popped out, I _____.

    relaxed   screamed   yawned

4. He won the race because he ran _____.

    quietly   noisily   fast

5. The squirrel gathers nuts because it will soon be _____.

    winter   hot   Friday

6. The people clapped because the show was _____.

    good   boring   strange

7. Because the girls are sisters, they look _____.

    hot   tired   alike

8. We can plant the flowers because it is _____.

    snowing   spring   dark

Just for Fun! Write to tell why this happened.
Everyone clapped and cheered!

Write a word from the Word Box to complete each sentence.

Word Box

brush	helping	tight	hungry
sticky	practice	warmer	birthday

I hope you'll like this gift!

1. I can't open the jar because the lid is too _____ .

2. Turn on the heater so the room will get _____ .

3. The paste makes my fingers _____ .

4. She gave me a gift because it is my _____ .

5. The smell of dinner cooking makes me feel _____ .

6. Dad thanked me for _____ with the dishes.

7. I play the piano better because I _____ each day.

8. I have no cavities because I _____ my teeth.

Just for Fun! Write to tell the reason this happened.
The frog jumped on the lily pad.

66   FS-32028 Critical Thinking

Name _____

Write a phrase from the Word Box to complete each sentence.

Word Box

is too high	it is winter
I was sleepy	smiled at him
did not eat breakfast	had a haircut
it is spring	he is ill

1. My hair was too long so I _____ .

2. I am hungry because I _____ .

3. I went to bed early because _____ .

4. The baby smiled when I _____ .

5. Matt is absent because _____ .

6. Flowers are growing because _____ .

7. Nights are cold because _____ .

8. I need the ladder because the shelf _____ .

Just for Fun! Write to show the reason this happened.
The kitten hid under the basket.

     FS-32028 Critical Thinking

Name _____

Circle the correct word.
Then write the word on the line
to complete each sentence.

1. I studied because I want my score to be _____ .

                        good   neat   hard

2. She takes turns because she is _____ .

                old   fair   funny

3. My best friend is absent, so I am _____ .

             happy   angry   lonely

4. Mother is taking a nap because she is _____ .

               tired   silly   relaxed

5. I cross in the crosswalk because it is _____ .

              fun   dangerous   safe

6. My tooth is aching, so I will see the _____ .

             movie   dentist   vet

7. Dad worried because I was _____ .

            early   friendly   late

8. I like stuffed animals because they are _____ .

             scary   cuddly   hard

9. My mouth puckered because the lemon was _____ .

              sweet   sour   wet

10. We need new tires because these are _____ .

             black   thick   worn

Just for Fun! Write to show what happened next.
He put in too much air in the big balloon.

                FS-32028 Critical Thinking

Write a word from the Word Box to complete each sentence.

Word Box

| late | forgot | dark | broken |
| young | excited | hurt | defrost |

1. I can't buy milk because I _____ my money.

2. I need to borrow a pencil because mine is _____ .

3. We can't watch that show because it is on too _____ .

4. My baby sister can't talk because she is too _____ .

5. I turned on the lamp because the room was _____ .

6. Loud music makes my ears _____ .

7. I took the meat out of the freezer so it could _____ .

8. The girl raised her voice because she was _____ .

Just for Fun! Write to tell the reason this happened.
The girl has mud on her shoes.

FS-32028 Critical Thinking

Name _____ Skill: Determining cause and effect

Write a phrase from the Word Box to complete each sentence.

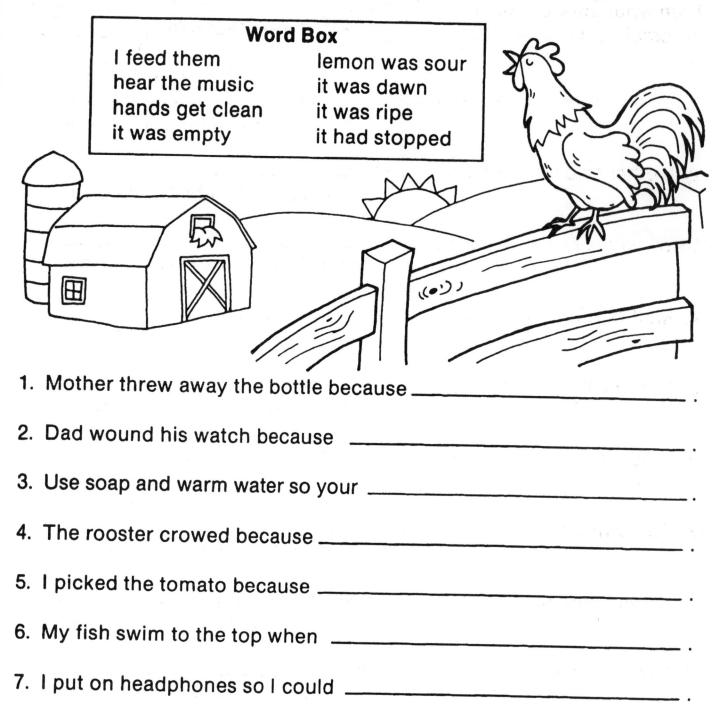

Word Box

I feed them   lemon was sour
hear the music   it was dawn
hands get clean   it was ripe
it was empty   it had stopped

1. Mother threw away the bottle because _____ .

2. Dad wound his watch because _____ .

3. Use soap and warm water so your _____ .

4. The rooster crowed because _____ .

5. I picked the tomato because _____ .

6. My fish swim to the top when _____ .

7. I put on headphones so I could _____ .

8. My mouth puckered up because the _____ .

Just for Fun! Write to show what happened next.
The pig was rolling in the mud.

FS-32028 Critical Thinking

Circle the correct word.
Then write the word on the line
to complete each sentence.

Mom, can you fix my new toy?

1. I want to buy an ice cream cone, so I need _____ .

   spoons   money   pins

2. Mother said thank you because I _____ .

   played   laughed   helped

3. When the new toy broke, I was _____ .

   disappointed   hungry   friendly

4. Mother is late, so I must _____ .

   laugh   wait   talk

5. The smell of cookies baking made me _____ .

   sad   eat   hungry

6. When the ice cream was left on the table, it _____ .

   melted   froze   cooked

7. There was no traffic, so she arrived _____ .

   late   early   quietly

8. If you jump from the ladder you could get _____ .

   bigger   heavy   hurt

9. I can't lift the box because it is too _____ .

   dry   light   heavy

10. That mask is scary because it is _____ .

   ugly   heavy   pretty

Just for Fun! Write to show what happened next.
The hot air balloon landed on the playground.

So...

Write a phrase from the box at the right to tell what *most likely* happened as a result of the action.

1. The telephone rang so

   _____

   _____

| I answered it. |
| I hung up. |
| it was loud. |

2. My friend got sick yesterday so

   _____

   _____

| he rode his bike to school. |
| he felt better. |
| he was absent today. |

3. We were noisy during the fire drill so

   _____

   _____

| we talked too much. |
| we had to do it over. |
| we had a real fire. |

4. At camp we left food on the picnic table so

   _____

   _____

| Dad cooked it. |
| the animals ate it. |
| it would taste better. |

5. I lost my lunch money on the way to school so

   _____

   _____

| it's probably on the bus. |
| I had to borrow money. |
| I ate the lunch I packed. |

6. Jerry is allergic to seafood so

   _____

   _____

   _____

| he doesn't go to aquariums. |
| he always asks what's in the food he's served. |
| he never eats vegetables. |

Try This! Complete this sentence with four different results: I just won the watermelon-eating contest at the fair so...

 FS-32028 Critical Thinking

Name _____ Date _____

Swimming Champ

If insects had Olympic Games, the backswimmer would be the champ. It could easily win all the swimming medals.

Backswimmers are water bugs that live in ponds. They spend all their lives on their backs. Their back legs are twice as long as their front legs. The back legs are used as paddles. Backswimmers can swim very fast. Whenever they are in danger, they swim to the bottom. They can hardly walk on land but they are good fliers.

Backswimmers can stay under the water for a long time. When they need air, they stick out their stomachs. Air flows in and is trapped in the stomach hairs. It forms a small air bubble. Then the backswimmer swims under the water again.
A backswimmer's bite is deadly to other insects and small fish. It has poison in it. The bite won't kill a person but is very painful.

1. Who do backswimmers kill with their bite?

_____

2. What part of their bodies do they use for

swimming? _____

3. Where do backswimmers live? _____

4. When do backswimmers swim to the

bottom? _____

5. Why don't backswimmers spend much

time on land? _____

_____

6. How do backswimmers breathe under

water? _____

Brainwork! Think about the question. Write the answer on the back.
Imagine you were holding an Animal Olympics. List the animals you would **enter**.

The Walking Stick

How would you like to have a pet snake? You say that doesn't sound very interesting? How about a stick that moves?

Large stick-insects are brown and look just like twigs. The small ones are green and look like blades of grass. When they stand still, they are almost impossible to see. During the day they "play dead". You can move their legs in any direction. They will stay that way for the rest of the day. Stick-insects feed and move around at night. They live in trees and eat leaves. At night, their skin color gets darker.

Only a few stick-insects have wings. They usually keep them folded away. But if a bird chases them, they will spread their wings. The wings flash a bright color. That surprises the bird. Then the stick-insect flies to another tree. It stands still and seems to disappear.

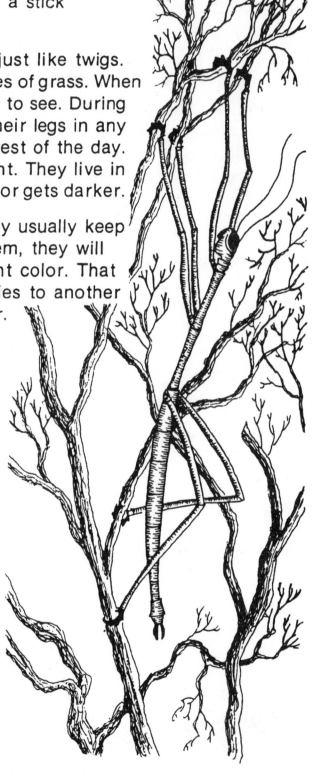

1. Who looks like a blade of grass?

_____

2. What do stick-insects eat? _____

_____

3. Where do stick-insects live?

_____

4. When do stick-insects "play dead"?

_____

5. Why are stick-insects hard to see?

_____

6. How do stick-insects surprise birds?

_____

_____

FS-32028 Critical Thinking

Flying Ghosts

Did you ever see a ghost that looked like a bird? In South America, some people are afraid of the oilbird . They think the bird's call sounds like a dead man crying.

Oilbirds spend all their lives in darkness. During the day they live in dark caves. Not one ray of light shines through. The oilbird's legs are too weak to stand on. Instead, they hang onto the walls of the caves. They fly back and forth without bumping into the walls. As they fly, they make a clicking sound. The sound bounces off the walls. The bird can "hear" where the walls are. Once a scientist put some cotton in an oilbird's ears. The bird became helpless and crashed into the walls. When the cotton was taken out, the bird didn't hit the walls once.

Oilbirds fly out of their caves at night. They will fly up to 50 miles in search of fruit, their favorite food.

1. **Who put the cotton in the oilbird's ears?**

   _____

2. **What do some people think the oilbird**

   sounds like? _____

3. **Where do oilbirds live?** _____

   _____

4. **When do oilbirds leave their caves?** ____

   _____

5. **Why is an oilbird's hearing so important?**

   _____

6. **How far will an oilbird travel for food?**

   _____

Brainwork! Think about the question. Write the answer on the back.
How do people who cannot see get around without bumping into things?

Mermaids or Monsters?

Sailors used to tell stories about beautiful women with fish tails. They were called mermaids. Christopher Columbus once thought he saw one. The next day he found out it was only a manatee. Today it is hard to believe anyone could make such a mistake. A manatee looks more like a floating log.

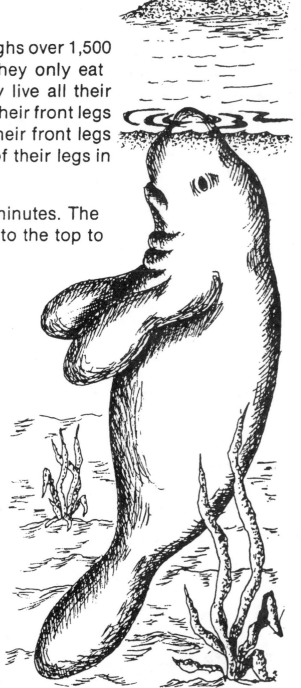

A manatee is huge. It is 15 feet long and weighs over 1,500 pounds. But manatees are gentle animals. They only eat water weeds—about 100 pounds a day! They live all their lives in the water. Their tails are like shovels. Their front legs are shaped like paddles. Manatees can use their front legs like hands. Sometimes they walk on the tips of their legs in shallow water.

Manatees can stay under the water for 16 minutes. The babies are born underwater. Then they swim to the top to take their first breath.

1. **Who thought the manatee looked like mermaids?** _____

2. **What does a manatee eat?** _____

    _____

3. **Where are baby manatees born?** _____

    _____

4. **When do baby manatees take their first**

    breath? _____

5. **Why did sailors tell stories?** _____

    _____

6. **How long can a manatee stay underwater?**

    _____

Brainwork! Think about the question. Write the answer on the back. What does a manatee look like to you?

 FS-32028 Critical Thinking

Laughing Bird

If kookaburras went to school, they would probably always be in trouble. These birds never seem to stop making noise. The kookaburras laugh, scream and even bark. They usually call out at dawn or sunset. For that reason, some people call them clockbirds.

The kookaburra lives in Australia. It lives in the forest in small groups. Kookaburras are very friendly. They will accept food from people. Sometimes they even tap on windows to be fed. Kookaburras eat insects, crabs, fish and small birds. They are also quite famous as snake killers. A kookaburra will grab a snake behind its head. Then the kookaburra flies up very high and drops the snake. Kookaburras are sometimes very rude. Once a man riding through the forest fell off his horse. Two kookaburras in a nearby tree began to laugh very loudly.

1. Who made the two kookaburras laugh?

_____

2. What do kookaburras eat? _____

_____

3. Where do kookaburras live? _____

_____

4. When do kookaburras call out? _____

_____

5. Why are kookaburras friendly to people?

_____

6. How do kookaburras catch snakes? ___

_____

Brainwork! Think about the question. Write the answer on the back. What would be some of the problems of having a kookaburra?

FS-32028 Critical Thinking

Name _____ Date _____

Super Mom

The Surinam toad is the Super Mom of the animal world. What other animal would carry 60 kids on her back for four months?

The Surinam toad is only four inches long. Its flat body looks like a square pancake. Its head is shaped like a triangle. It has no tongue or teeth. This toad has touch organs on its fingers. These organs help the toad find food even in black mud. The toad uses its front feet to catch food. Then it pushes the food into its mouth. Surinam toads are strong swimmers. They spend most of their lives in water.

Just before the female lays her eggs, her skin becomes very soft. As she lays her eggs, she turns over in the water. The eggs sink into her back. The skin swells and a hole forms around each egg. Then a lid closes over each egg. After four months the lids open. The young toads swim out into the new world.

1. Who lives on the Surinam toad's back?

   _____

2. What does the Surinam toad use to find

   food? _____

3. Where does the Surinam toad live? ____

   _____

4. When does a female toad's skin become

   soft? _____

5. Why does the female turn over in the

   water? _____

6. How long is a Surinam toad? _____

Brainwork! Think about the question. Write the answer on the back. What would happen to the baby toads if they weren't carried on their mother's back?

FS-32028 Critical Thinking

Walking on Water

Basilisk lizards know a great trick. They can walk on water! The basilisk is found in South America and Mexico. In Mexico, these amazing animals are called "river runners". The male basilisk has a crest of skin on top. The crest goes from its head down to its back. Its toes are covered with small scales.

Basilisks live in bushes and trees near water. When they are frightened by another animal, they drop into the water. Sometimes they go straight down to the bottom. Other times they start running very quickly across the water. They run so fast they don't sink down. After running several feet, they slow down and begin swimming. The lizard's weight and scaly feet may keep it from sinking down.

Basilisks lay 20 eggs at a time. Afterwards, they cover the eggs with soil and leaves. The eggs hatch in three months. You can usually tell when a basilisk is relaxed. It wags its tail like a dog.

1. **Who has a crest of skin on top?** _____
_____

2. **What does the basilisk have on its toes?**
_____

3. **Where does the basilisk live?** _____
_____

4. **When does a basilisk drop into the water?**
_____

5. **Why is the basilisk so amazing?** _____
_____

6. **How many eggs does a basilisk lay?** ____
_____

Brainwork! Think about the question. Write the answer on the back. Why can't people walk on water?

Gecko in the House

Would you like a dinner guest who climbed the walls? No way, you say! In that case, don't invite a gecko!

Geckos are small lizards. They live in warm countries. Tree geckos seem to enjoy living in people's houses. Many people like geckos because they eat all the insects in the house. A gecko will go anywhere for a meal, even the ceiling! They have small hooks on the bottoms of their toes. Some geckos also have hooks on their tails. The hooks allow the gecko to climb even up glass walls. To unhook themselves, geckos curl and uncurl their toes. They can do this faster than an eye blinks.

Geckos can throw off their tails and grow new ones. Sometimes only part of the tail is thrown off. As a new tail grows, the old one heals. There have been two-tailed and even three-tailed geckos!

1. **Who can climb up your walls?** _____

_____

2. **What do geckos eat?** _____

3. **Where do geckos like to live?** _____

_____

4. **When do geckos climb up walls?** _____

_____

5. **Why do people like geckos?** _____

_____

6. **How do geckos climb up walls?** _____

_____

Brainwork! Think about the question. Write the answer on the back. Imagine that you could climb up walls. What would be good about it?

A Snaky Animal

It has a long, skinny neck that moves from side to side. When it finds something to eat, it strikes out. Then it swallows the dinner in one gulp. It's a snake, right? No, it's a turtle!

Snake-necked turtles are probably the world's strangest looking turtles. They live in South America and Australia. Their necks are sometimes as long as their bodies! Most of them cannot put their necks inside their shells. They just wrap their necks around their shells.

The snake-necked turtle lives in fresh water. It can swim underwater for a long time. To breathe, it keeps its nose just above the water. These turtles eat fish.

One kind of snake-necked turtle is called the "stinker". When it gets upset, it gives off a rotten smell. You can be sure that other animals leave the stinker alone.

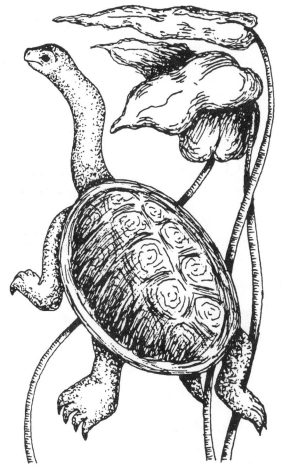

1. Who gives off a bad smell? _____

2. What kind of neck does a snake-necked

   turtle have? _____

3. Where do snake-necked turtles live? ___

   _____

4. When does the snake-necked turtle strike

   out with its neck? _____

   _____

5. Why can't these turtles put their necks

   inside their shells? _____

6. How does this turtle breathe underwater?

   _____

Brainwork! Think about the question. Write the answer on the back.
Make a list of at least five animals that have long necks.

 FS-32028 Critical Thinking

Name _____ Date _____

Deadly Snake

Many strange stories are told about the anaconda snake. Some people say it turns into a ship with sails at night. Others believe that the anaconda can swallow a man in one gulp.

Most of these stories are just tall tales. However, the anaconda really is one of the world's most dangerous animals. It is the largest of all snakes. The longest anaconda ever found was 37 feet long! Anacondas live in South America.

During the day these snakes sleep in tree branches. They move slowly on land. Anacondas can swim very quickly. They wait for an animal to come near the water's edge. Then they wind themselves around its body and drag it into the water. They hold the animal under the water until it drowns. Then they swallow the animal whole. Anacondas eat birds, fish, deer and even alligators. After a big meal, an anaconda snake will not move for a week.

1. Who can swallow an alligator whole?

_____

2. What did some people think an anaconda

   turned into at night? _____

3. Where do anacondas catch their dinners?

_____

4. When do anacondas sleep? _____

5. Why are people afraid of anacondas?

_____

6. How long will an anaconda rest after one

   meal? _____

Brainwork! Think about the question. Write the answer on the back. Write a one-paragraph story about an anaconda.

FS-32028 Critical Thinking

Eyeglasses for a Tapir?

Some people think the tapir needs glasses. It is always bumping into things. Tapirs, however, can see very well. They just never look where they are going. Tapirs have escape paths marked off in the bushes. When a tiger chases them, tapirs run away without looking in front of them. Once a tapir crashed right into a canoe.

Tapirs are found in South America and Asia. They live near lakes, streams or ponds. They are good swimmers and love taking mud baths.

When baby tapirs are born they are covered with spots and stripes. These markings disappear as the animals grow. The most important part of the tapir's body is its trunk. It uses its trunk to sniff out food. Scientists think the trunk may often save the tapir's life. It may be able to smell dangerous animals before they get too close.

1. **Who can scare a tapir?** _____

2. **What is the most important part of the**

   tapir's body? _____

3. **Where do tapirs live?** _____

   _____

4. **When are tapirs covered with stripes and**

   spots? _____

5. **Why do tapirs always bump into things?**

   _____

6. **How do tapirs protect themselves from**

   dangerous animals? _____

   _____

Brainwork! Think about the question. Write the answer on the back. Which sense is the most important to you: smell, taste, sight, hearing or touch? Why?

83   FS-32028 Critical Thinking

Life Upside Down

Would you like to spend your whole life upside-down? Well, the sloth seems to enjoy it. The sloth eats, sleeps and moves upside-down. It lives in the treetops of South America. It hangs onto branches with its long, sharp claws.

Everything about the sloth seems to be backwards. Even its hair grows backwards. The sloth can turn its head almost all the way around! It can raise its head up, while its body hangs down. The sloth hardly ever moves. When it does, it only goes one-third mile per hour. Some sloths live their entire lives in one tree! They eat fruits and leaves from the tree. Baby sloths are born upside-down. They hang onto their mother's stomach until they get big. Then they slowly move to another branch. Sloth mothers don't worry about the kids moving far from home.

1. **Who carries sloth babies on her**

   stomach? _____

2. **What do sloths eat?** _____

   _____

3. **Where do sloths hang?** _____

4. **When do sloths hang upside-down?** _____

   _____

5. **Why do sloths have long, sharp claws?**

   _____

6. **How far can a sloth turn its head?** _____

   _____

Brainwork! Think about the question. Write the answer on the back. Sometimes people are called "slothful". What do you think that means?

The Biggest One of All

If you ever saw a 120-pound rat, you'd probably be scared. Don't worry. The capybara is not really a rat. Both the capybara and the rat are rodents. The capybara, however, is harmless. Some capybaras have even been trained as pets.

The capybara is the world's largest rodent. It's four feet long. It has reddish-brown hair and small eyes and ears. This animal is found in South America. It eats water plants and grass.

Capybaras are super swimmers. Their feet are webbed like ducks' feet. They dive and swim far distances under water. When they are frightened, they will run like horses. Then they will jump into the nearest river. When they swim above water, only their eyes, ears and noses show. Capybaras can't stay out of water too long. If they do, their skin dries out. Since they like water so much, capybaras are sometimes called water pigs.

1. What do capybaras look like? _____

2. What do capybaras eat? _____

_____

3. Where are capybaras found? _____

_____

4. When do capybaras run like horses? ___

_____

5. Why must capybaras live near water? __

_____

6. How much do capybaras weigh? _____

_____

Brainwork! Think about the question. Write the answer on the back. Do you think a capybara would make a good pet? Why or why not?

FS-32028 Critical Thinking

Facts tell something that
is true. You can prove it!

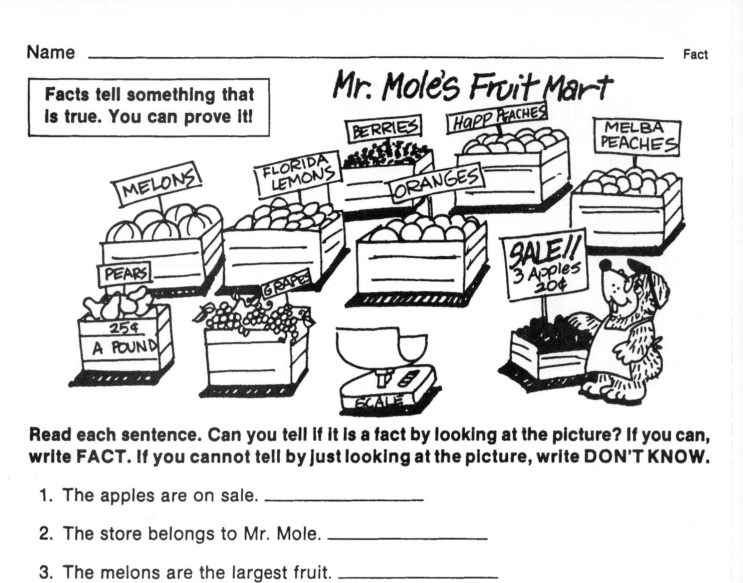

Read each sentence. Can you tell if it is a fact by looking at the picture? If you can, write FACT. If you cannot tell by just looking at the picture, write DON'T KNOW.

1. The apples are on sale. _____

2. The store belongs to Mr. Mole. _____

3. The melons are the largest fruit. _____

4. The pears are ripe. _____

5. There are two kinds of peaches. _____

6. Mr. Mole is a father. _____

7. There is a scale. _____

8. The fruit was picked yesterday. _____

Answer these questions with a fact.

9. How much do pears cost? _____

10. Where is Mr. Mole's hand? _____

11. Where are the lemons from? _____

★ **Why do you think the apples are on sale?**

86   FS-32028 Critical Thinking

Learn Some Facts!

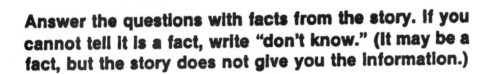

"I want to take a ride on the roller coaster, Dad!" shouted Eric. "I love fast rides!"

"Let's find out if it's safe first," said Dad. Dad walked up to a booth. He asked for information about the Speeding Bullet ride.

"It's very safe," the man said. "We check it every day. The Speeding Bullet was built seven years ago. It goes 50 miles an hour. Pretty fast, but we've never had an accident."

Eric could hardly wait for the ride to start. Dad grabbed the bar. He closed his eyes and didn't open them again. Whoosh! Zoom! Whee! Yikes! Eric loved the Speeding Bullet. He wanted to go again. "Not a chance," Dad said, shaking. "We're going on the merry-go-round. I like nice, slow horses."

Answer the questions with facts from the story. If you cannot tell it is a fact, write "don't know." (It may be a fact, but the story does not give you the information.)

1. What is the name of the ride?

_____

2. Of what is the Speeding Bullet made?

_____

3. When was the Speeding Bullet built?

_____

4. How much do the tickets cost?

_____

5. How long did the ride last?

_____

6. Why did Dad want to ride the merry-go-round?

_____

★ Look at the picture. How do you think Dad feels?

87

Newspapers can give you the **facts** of a story.

Where Are The Facts?

Children Want Park
by Rich Andrews

Early Monday morning, 50 children marched into the mayor's office. "We need a place to play!" they all said.

"There is no empty land to build a park," answered the mayor. "But let me talk to my friends. Maybe we can think of something for you." Two weeks went by. The children had to play on the sidewalks. It was too crowded to even throw a ball.

Late one night, David Lopez heard something outside his window. He saw some men putting up fences across each end of the street. They hung up a sign: "CHILDREN'S PARK—NO CARS ALLOWED". At last, the children had a place to play.

If the sentence is a fact, write FACT. If it is not a fact stated in the story, write DK ("don't know").

1. All sidewalks are crowded. _____

2. David Lopez can sing. _____

3. The children wanted a park. _____

4. Some men put up a fence. _____

5. There is no empty land. _____

6. A sign said, "CHILDREN'S PARK". _____

7. Why did the children want a park?

_____

8. When did the children go see the mayor?

_____

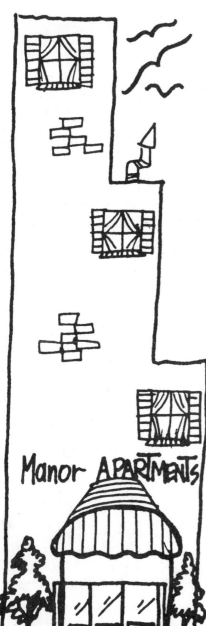

Manor APARTMENTS

★ **Where do you think all the children lived?**

88

Check for Facts

Read each sentence. If it is a fact, write F. Check the story. Some questions you cannot answer. There are not enough facts. Write DK ("don't know") on the line.

1. Peter is president of the club. _____

2. Fred is not a club member. _____

3. The meeting is on Tuesday. _____

4. Only boys belong to the club. _____

5. Fred lives at 8320 Clook Lane. _____

6. Peter is smarter than Chuck. _____

7. Chuck checked his facts by looking _____ .

★ **Why do you think Fred is not a member of the club?**

A **fact** tells something that is true. You can prove it.

Look at each picture carefully. If a sentence is a fact, write FACT. You must prove it by looking at the picture. If you cannot prove the sentence is a fact, write DK ("don't know").

1. Sarah is talking on the phone. _____

2. The phone is on the table. _____

3. The man is Sarah's father. _____

4. A note is on the desk. _____

5. The man is very tall. _____

6. The man bought his pen. _____

Answer the questions.

7. "It has two flowers on it" would

   be a fact about: _____

8. "It is a fruit" would be a fact about:

   _____

9. Write a fact about Sarah: _____

   _____

10. Write a fact about the clock: ____

    _____

11. "It is broken" is a fact about:

    _____

12. Write a fact about the man's suit:

    _____

★ **What do you think Sarah is talking about?**

90   FS-32028 Critical Thinking

How Can You Prove Facts?

Information books can give you
facts about different things.

"We're studying about winter in our class," Dennis
told his dad. "I need to do a report on how animals sleep.
Where can I find out about that?"

Dad drove Dennis to the library. "Here's a book that
will help you. Turn to page 22." Dennis read the story.

Many animals sleep all winter long. Some
sleep in caves. Other animals sleep under
the ground. Their bodies get very, very
cold. This does not hurt them. When spring
comes, the animals start moving around.
They are very hungry. The animals hunt for
food until winter comes again.

Answer each question with a fact.

1. **What does an information book give you?**

   _____

2. **How long do many animals sleep?**

   _____

3. **Where did Dennis find his information?**

   _____

4. **How do the animals feel in spring?**

   _____

5. **Name two places where animals sleep.**

   _____

6. **Write two facts about the picture above.**

_____

_____

★**What do you think is the most interesting part of the animal story?**

91   FS-32028 Critical Thinking

A fact tells something
that is true.

"It's getting late," Julie told her sister. "Let's hurry home." Julie and Sue left the park. They walked four blocks up Pine Street. It was getting darker and darker. There were no lights on the street.

A big round moon rose in the sky. The night was very still and quiet. Julie and Sue walked faster and faster. "See that orange and white building?" Sue pointed. "That's where we turn." When the girls came to the corner, Julie saw something move. Slowly, it came closer and closer. It was a shadow. Julie grabbed Sue's arm and started to run.

"I've been waiting for you girls," a voice shouted. "Come back!" Julie was so frightened, she tripped and fell. "Are you all right? Why did you run away?" the voice asked.

"Oh, Dad! It's you! Your shadow scared us!"

Find the facts. Answer each question with a complete sentence.

1. Who are Julie and Sue?

_____

2. What color is the building?

_____

3. How does the moon look?

_____

4. Where had the girls been playing?

_____

5. On what street did the girls walk?

_____

★ **Look at the picture. Why does a shadow seem very scary?**

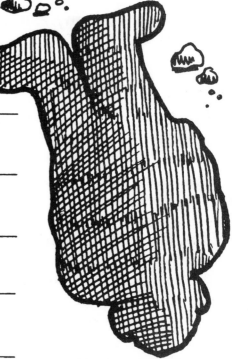

FS-32028 Critical Thinking

Opinion words
to watch for:
seems
thinks
looks
feels
thought

Do you like this
kind of cereal?

**An opinion tells how you
feel about something.**

It looks a little
mushy to me. I don't
think I'll like it.

Read the letter. Underline the opinion words you find.

Dear Patti,

It has been two weeks since we moved. I sure miss my friends in
Lake View. I feel very lonely. Yesterday, my mother took me to
Sunset Park. She thought I would meet someone to play with. I
didn't, though.

My new school seems to be a lot bigger than Dover Street. It has more
swings and climbing bars. School opens in four days. I think I'll go down
and meet my new teacher on Thursday. We're coming back to Lake View
for Thanksgiving. I'll be staying at my grandmother's. I hope you will
come see me. Write soon.

Love, Anna

1. **Why does Anna feel lonely?**

_____

2. **Why does the new school seem bigger?**

_____

3. **What does Anna think she should do on Thursday?**

_____

4. **How do you think Anna could meet new friends?**

_____

5. **Would you like to go to a new school? Tell why or why not.**

We use the words in the box below with opinion words. They tell how we feel about people and things: Joe **thinks** Judy is funny.

More Opinion Words
angry   sad   worried   happy   funny   pretty   strange   nice   proud

(1)Write how you think each person below feels. (2) Tell why you think the person feels that way. Use opinion words in your answers.

1. Joan: (1) _____

             (2) _____

2. Marvin: (1) _____

             (2) _____

3. Thomas: (1) _____

             (2) _____

4. Mother: (1) _____

             (2) _____

94   FS-32028 Critical Thinking

In My Opinion...

Answer each question in a complete sentence.

1. Why do you think Mrs. Potter is angry?

_____

2. What seems to be making Sally feel sad?

_____

3. What has happened to the plant? How do you think it happened?

_____

4. In the picture, who looks very smart? What makes you think so?

_____

5. Why do you think John is not doing his work?

_____

6. How do you think Lauri is feeling? Tell why.

_____

People have different opinions about the same thing. Read Meg and Neal's opinions about homework. Are their opinions the same?

I love it!

That's awful!

It's so-so

It looks strange to me!

My teacher gave us three pages of homework today. I like homework. It helps me to learn better. Sometimes I don't finish my work at night. So I get up real early and do it. I'm getting smarter and smarter.

Homework takes too much time. I'm too busy to do it. In the afternoon, I have to play. At night, I have to watch "That's Amazing!" I guess I could do homework at 10 p.m., but I'm too tired then. My teacher is nice, but I wish he wouldn't give homework.

1. Meg thinks homework will:
   a. help her sleep better
   b. help her think better
   c. help her learn better

2. Neal feels that homework:
   a. is better than playing
   b. takes too much time
   c. makes him tired

3. How does Neal feel about his teacher?

_____

4. What is your opinion about Neal?

_____

5. Why do you think teachers give homework?

_____

6. Are you like Meg or Neal? Why?

_____

   FS-32028 Critical Thinking

Opinion Words

seems
think
feel
looks
should

1. **What is Ron's opinion about salt water?**

_____

2. **Why does Ron like the mountains?**

_____

3. **Why doesn't Nina think the mountains are peaceful?**

_____

4. **Do you think Nina should go to the mountains? Tell why or why not.**

_____

5. **Nina does not like mountain noises. What could she
do so she wouldn't hear them?**

_____

More Opinion Words

pretty	best	funny	nice
great	smart	worst	awful
good	kind	mean	angry

Think about the person whose name is in dark print. Write your opinion about them. Use an opinion word from the box above.

1. **Jason** would not give Terry a cookie.
   He ate all of them by himself.

   _____

2. **Dave's** pizza is made with lots of cheese.
   Everyone loves to eat it!

   _____

3. **Michelle** told a joke.
   Everyone laughed and laughed.

   _____

4. **Mrs. Ellis** picked up the lost kitten.
   She gave him some warm milk.

   _____

5. **Brian** slammed the door.
   He wouldn't speak to anyone.

   _____

6. **Lynn** is wearing a beautiful dress.
   Her dad wants to take her picture.

   _____

FS-32028 Critical Thinking

Who Dun It?

If the sentence is a fact, write FACT. You must be able to prove it by looking at the picture. If the sentence is an opinion, write OPINION.

1. Someone is hiding. _____

2. Detective Nelda is very smart. _____

3. Someone was reading a book. _____

4. A shoe is on the floor. _____

5. The picture is broken. _____

6. The curtains are pretty. _____

7. The thief is poor. _____

8. Write two facts about the thief. _____

_____

9. What makes you think it is nighttime? _____

_____

10. To whom do you think the shoe belongs? Tell why. _____

_____

99

Description of Barney O'Malley	
Eyes:	Brown
Hair:	Red
Height:	Five feet
Age:	12 years

Has anyone seen this boy? Farmer Rooney is looking for him. He thinks Barney took his prize rooster, Rocky.

"Barney never, ever gets up on time for school," Farmer Rooney explained. "He is always late. That makes his teacher very angry. Barney doesn't like alarm clocks. He wakes up feeling crabby.

"Rocky is a great rooster. He cock-a-doodles and he sings, too. He knows lots of songs— Twinkle Little Star; Row Your Boat. I sure miss ol' Rocky. He crowed when it was time for me to get up. I always knew when it was 6 a.m. H-m-m-m. I've got an idea. I'll put Rocky's voice on tape. Barney can put the tape inside his clock. Then we'll both get up on time!"

If the sentence is a fact, write FACT. If it is an opinion, write OPINION.

1. Rocky is a rooster. _____

2. Farmer Rooney is sad. _____

3. Barney's teacher is nice. _____

4. Some clocks have alarms. _____

5. Rocky is a very good singer. _____

6. Barney has red hair. _____

7. Barney is always late. _____

Answer each question.

8. Do you think Farmer Rooney has a clock? Tell why or why not.

_____

9. How does Barney feel about alarms? Tell why.

_____

10. Why do you think Barney has such a hard time waking up?

_____

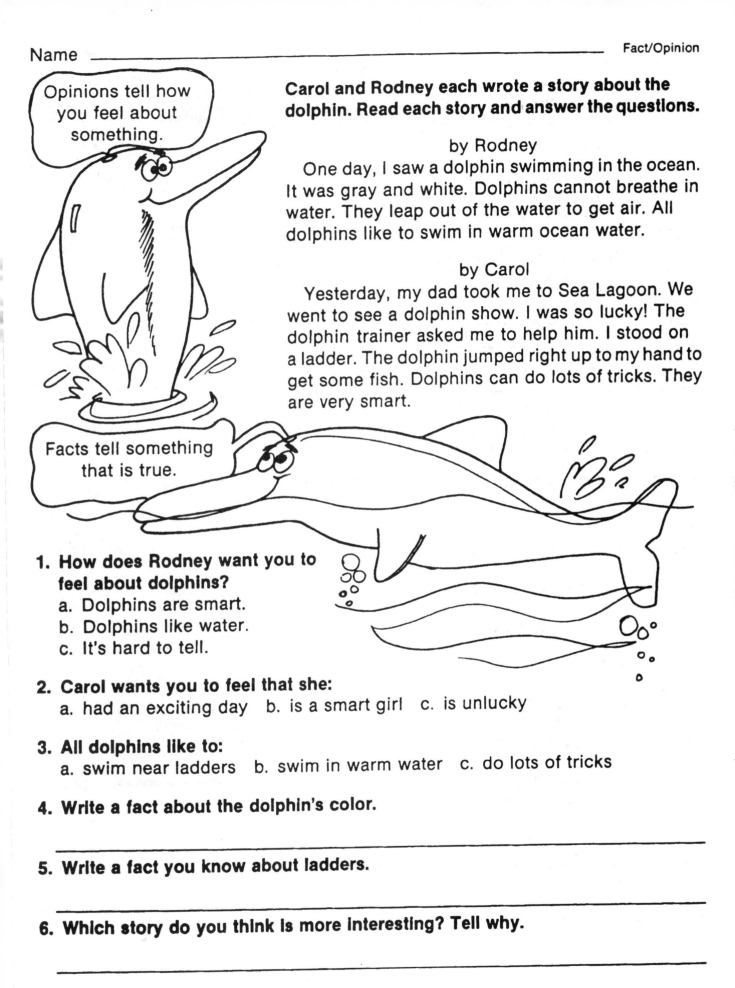

Opinions tell how you feel about something.

Carol and Rodney each wrote a story about the dolphin. Read each story and answer the questions.

by Rodney
One day, I saw a dolphin swimming in the ocean. It was gray and white. Dolphins cannot breathe in water. They leap out of the water to get air. All dolphins like to swim in warm ocean water.

by Carol
Yesterday, my dad took me to Sea Lagoon. We went to see a dolphin show. I was so lucky! The dolphin trainer asked me to help him. I stood on a ladder. The dolphin jumped right up to my hand to get some fish. Dolphins can do lots of tricks. They are very smart.

Facts tell something that is true.

1. **How does Rodney want you to feel about dolphins?**
   a. Dolphins are smart.
   b. Dolphins like water.
   c. It's hard to tell.

2. **Carol wants you to feel that she:**
   a. had an exciting day   b. is a smart girl   c. is unlucky

3. **All dolphins like to:**
   a. swim near ladders   b. swim in warm water   c. do lots of tricks

4. **Write a fact about the dolphin's color.**

   _____

5. **Write a fact you know about ladders.**

   _____

6. **Which story do you think is more interesting? Tell why.**

   _____

101   FS-32028 Critical Thinking

Ads can tell facts and opinions.

...AND NOW A WORD ABOUT RAZZLE-DAZZLE GUM FROM ME, PERCY QUINN...

"Do you want to taste something really special? Try Razzle-Dazzle Bubble Gum— the gum with zap! and zing! It'll wake up your mouth. Razzle-Dazzle comes in four flavors: cherry, grape, tooty-frooty, and red hot pepper. As I unwrap the paper, I can smell those peppers! Sniff! M-m-m-m!

"Now, here's the surprise. You can blow square bubbles with Razzle-Dazzle. (Chew, chew, chew. Phoo, phoo. POP!) Isn't that terrific? I think blowing bubbles is more fun than anything!

"Rush out now and buy some Razzle-Dazzle. Each pack costs 25 cents. One little piece will make you feel like a new person. Hurry!"

Write whether each sentence is a FACT or Percy's OPINION.

1. Razzle-Dazzle is a gum. _____

2. Razzle-Dazzle comes in four flavors. _____

3. Red hot pepper is the best flavor. _____

4. Razzle-Dazzle has zing! _____

5. Razzle-Dazzle costs 25 cents. _____

6. Blowing bubbles is fun! _____

7. What do you think of Percy's clothes?

_____

8. Would you buy Razzle-Dazzle Gum? Tell why or why not.

_____

9. What is your favorite food? Tell me why I should like it.

_____

Who is Right?

Read both stories then answer the questions.

Eric

My favorite place is on Clover street. It is Mrs. Mays' Mart. She has all my favorite foods: apples, bananas, hot dogs, and chocolate milk. The Mart always smells like fresh peanuts and I love peanuts! Small markets are best. You never have to wait in line.

Bonnie

My favorite place is the brown and green AMB super store. They have the best oatmeal cookies—the kind that are so-o-o soft. Big markets are the best! They have so many foods and so many people.

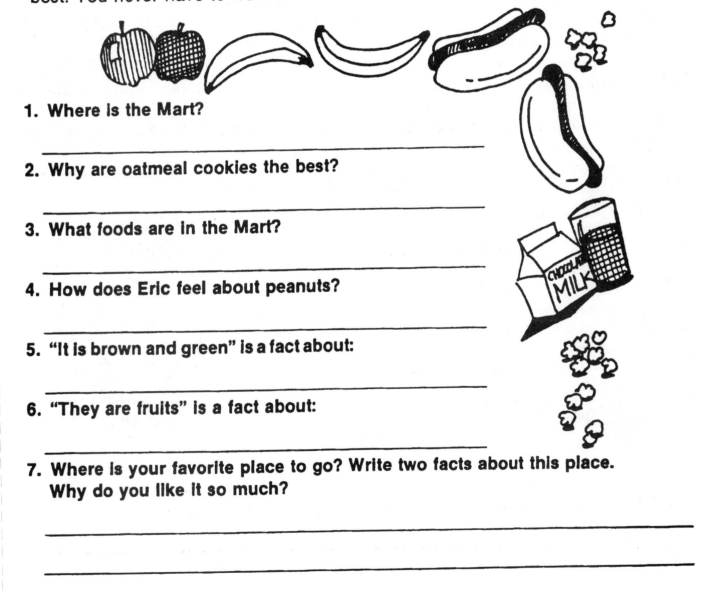

1. Where is the Mart?

_____

2. Why are oatmeal cookies the best?

_____

3. What foods are in the Mart?

_____

4. How does Eric feel about peanuts?

_____

5. "It is brown and green" is a fact about:

_____

6. "They are fruits" is a fact about:

_____

7. Where is your favorite place to go? Write two facts about this place. Why do you like it so much?

_____

_____

_____

"I love this kind of day," said Linda. "It makes me feel like being very quiet."

"Gray days make me feel sad," moaned Steven, putting on a sweater. "I like warm sunny days best. They make me feel happy."

"Look at that cloud over there," pointed Carol. "It has a tail and feet just like a duck, doesn't it?"

Linda looked at the cloud carefully. "I think it's an elephant. It has a long trunk hanging down."

Steven stared at the cloud a long time. "I have it! It's not a duck. It's not an elephant. It's a platypus!"

Look at the picture. If the sentence is a fact, write FACT. If you cannot tell, write DK.

1. Linda likes the grass. _____

2. The cloud has a tail. _____

3. The children are lost. _____

4. It is November. _____

5. Carol has a toy. _____

6. There is an apple tree. _____

7. Linda is wearing shoes. _____

8. It is early morning. _____

Answer each question.

9. Do you think Steven is cold? How can you tell?

_____

10. What does Linda think about the cloud?

_____

11. How does Steven feel about gray days?

_____

104

Answer Key

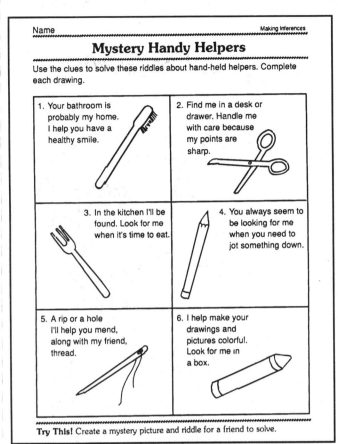

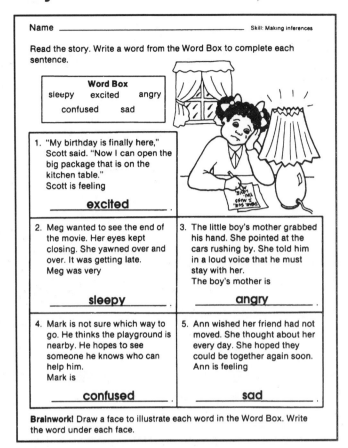

Page 1

Page 2

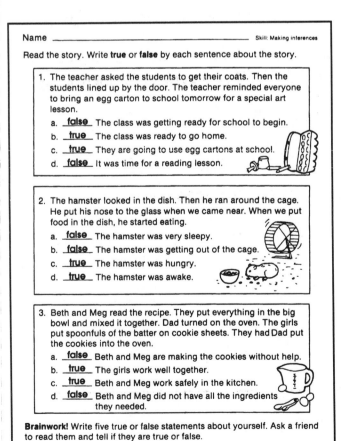

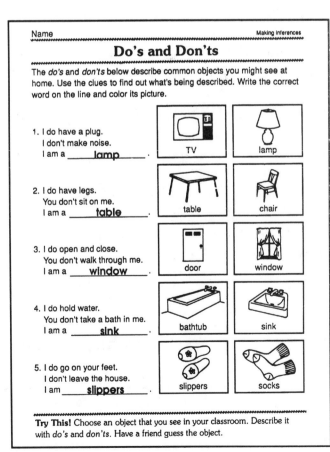

Page 3

Page 4

Answer Key

What Next?

Read the sentences about each picture. Decide what is *most likely* to happen next. Write your choice on the line.

1. The cake was finally cool. Bill got the knife and bowl of icing. What will happen next?

   • Bill will cut the cake.
   • Bill will spread the icing.

   Bill will spread the icing.

2. The sky became dark. Mark heard rumbling and saw flashes of light. What will happen next?

   • It will begin to rain.
   • The power will go out.

   It will begin to rain.

3. Tasha tossed the stick across the yard. Shaggy ran to get it. What will happen next?

   • Shaggy will bring it back to Tasha.
   • Tasha will toss a ball across the yard.

   Shaggy will bring it back to Tasha.

4. Mother Bird returned to her nest with a juicy worm. The babies' mouths were open. What will happen next?

   • Mother will eat the worm.
   • Mother will feed her babies.

   Mother will feed her babies.

Try This! For one of the stories above, write why you chose your answer.

Page 5

It Isn't

In each box below you are to find out what animal is described. One way to do this is by first deciding what animal it *isn't*. Read the clues. Use each animal's name only once to complete the sentences. Then follow the directions.

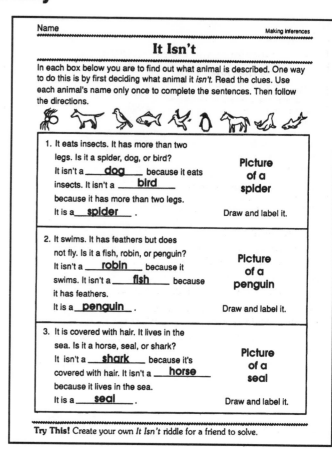

1. It eats insects. It has more than two legs. Is it a spider, dog, or bird?
   It isn't a __dog__ because it eats insects. It isn't a __bird__ because it has more than two legs.
   It is a __spider__.

   Picture of a spider

   Draw and label it.

2. It swims. It has feathers but does not fly. Is it a fish, robin, or penguin?
   It isn't a __robin__ because it swims. It isn't a __fish__ because it has feathers.
   It is a __penguin__.

   Picture of a penguin

   Draw and label it.

3. It is covered with hair. It lives in the sea. Is it a horse, seal, or shark?
   It isn't a __shark__ because it's covered with hair. It isn't a __horse__ because it lives in the sea.
   It is a __seal__.

   Picture of a seal

   Draw and label it.

Try This! Create your own *It Isn't* riddle for a friend to solve.

Page 6

Read the story. Write **true** or **false** by each sentence about the story.

1. Jeff wanted a pet. He went to the library to get out a book on cats. He wanted to find out how to take care of a kitten. Then he and his family would go to the animal shelter to get a kitten.

   a. __false__ Jeff does not know if he wants a cat or dog.
   b. __true__ Jeff wants to learn about kittens.
   c. __false__ Jeff went to the pet store.
   d. __false__ Jeff found a cat at the library.

2. Peter is glad the tree is big and strong. He wants to build a tree fort in it. Daddy will buy the wood for the fort early Saturday morning. Then they will start working on the fort.

   a. __false__ Peter hopes it rains Saturday.
   b. __false__ The tree was planted last week.
   c. __true__ The fort will be made of wood.
   d. __false__ Peter is building the fort by himself.

3. Cindi was looking forward to Friday night. She would use her new sleeping bag. She knew it was going to be fun staying at her best friend's house. She wondered what they would have for breakfast in the morning.

   a. __false__ Cindi is going camping.
   b. __true__ The sleeping bag has never been used.
   c. __true__ Cindi will stay overnight with her friend.
   d. __true__ Cindi will be at her friend's house on Saturday morning.

Brainwork! Make a list of things Cindi will take to her friend's house.

Page 7

Read the clues. Write the answer on the line.

1. I sleep in a crib.
   I drink from a bottle.
   I cannot walk or talk.
   Who am I?

   a baby

   a puppy, a baby, a clown

2. Put me on your feet.
   I will keep you warm and dry.
   Wear me when it rains.
   What am I?

   boots

   socks, shoes, boots

3. I grow on an ear.
   Cook me in hot oil.
   I will puff up and taste good.
   What am I?

   popcorn

   French fries, popcorn, a hot dog

4. Paste me on an envelope.
   You need me before you can mail a letter.
   What am I?

   a stamp

   a mailbox, a post card, a stamp

5. I have no color.
   You need me every day.
   You drink me when you are thirsty.
   What am I?

   water

   juice, water, milk

6. I look like a baby.
   You can give me a name.
   Children like to play with me.
   What am I?

   a doll

   a teddy bear, a doll, a ball

Brainwork! Write clues about an object. Ask a friend to guess the name of the object.

Page 8

Answer Key

Name _____ Skill: Making inferences

Read the story. Write the answers to the questions.

The Talent Show

The school talent show was going to be held again. Pam and Patti both circled the date on their calendars.

Pam practiced playing piano every day. Patti did her dance for the show over and over. She showed the dance to Pam at school on the playground.

The girls' families will get there early so that they can find seats in the front row. Last year at the end of the show, the audience clapped and cheered.

Possible answers

1. You can tell that the girls probably attended the same school because **they were on the playground together**

2. Why do you think there will be a lot of people watching the show? **Families will get there early to get seats.**

3. The reason Pam and Patti are practicing so much is **they want to perform well at the show**

4. When the girls found out about the show, they probably felt (silly, frightened, excited) **excited**

5. Before Patti dances at the show, she will probably be feeling (proud, nervous, angry) **nervous**

6. What clue word tells you the show has been held before? **again**

Brainwork! Make a picture about a school talent show.

Page 9

Name _____ Skill: Making inferences

Read the story and the two sentences after the story. Write the **true** sentence on the line.

1. Emily looked at the list. She put her things in the suitcase. She was happy that her friend was going with her. She knew they would have fun swimming, fishing and sleeping in a tent.
   a. Emily is going to school.
   b. She is going to camp.

   She is going to camp.

2. Mother pulled the car into the driveway. Then she rolled up all the windows. She wet the car and rubbed it with rags. Then she dried it off and cleaned the windows.
   a. Mother has a new car.
   b. She washed the car.

   She washed the car.

3. The boys put their money in their jacket pockets. They have saved enough to get Dad a nice gift. Now it is time to buy it. Dad will be surprised tonight.
   a. The boys are going shopping.
   b. The boys will get their favorite toys.

   The boys are going shopping.

4. Mother told everyone where to stand. Then she told everyone to be sure to smile. She made sure she could see everyone. Then she counted to three and pushed the button.
   a. Mother took a picture.
   b. Mother needs new glasses.

   Mother took a picture.

Brainwork! Draw and label five things the boys might buy for Dad.

Page 10

Name _____ Making inferences

Can You Tell?

Read the story and statements below carefully. Decide if each statement is true, false, or if you can't tell from the information given in the story. Fill in the correct circle beside each statement.

A Fresh Start

Greg was moving to a new town on September 4, just in time to start the year in a new school.

He wondered if he would be allowed to ride his bike to this school. He was too young last year. In his last school, only students ten or older could ride bikes to school.

He wondered who his new friends would be. Would they want to watch TV after school, or would they rather play outside like he does?

Greg's brother would be going to the same school. Greg decided they could help each other make new friends.

	True	False	Can't Tell
1. Greg will move in before school starts.	1. ●	○	○
2. Greg is ten years old.	2. ○	○	●
3. Greg would rather watch TV after school than play outside.	3. ○	●	○
4. Greg has an older brother.	4. ○	○	●
5. Greg rode his bike to school last year.	5. ○	●	○
6. Greg's new school starts in September.	6. ●	○	○
7. Greg is in third grade.	7. ○	○	●
8. Greg would like to ride his bike to school.	8. ●	○	○

Try This! Based on the story, write how you think Greg feels about moving.

Page 11

Name _____ Skill: Making inferences

Read the story. Write the answers to the questions.

Faraway Friends

Jane hoped to get another letter from Kim soon. Kim was in third grade also. Kim promised she would send a photograph of herself. It was fun to hear from someone who was living on an island in the United States where the weather is always warm. Jane wondered if Kim would like to play in the snow in her backyard in Michigan. Jane hoped that someday she would get to meet her **faraway friend.**

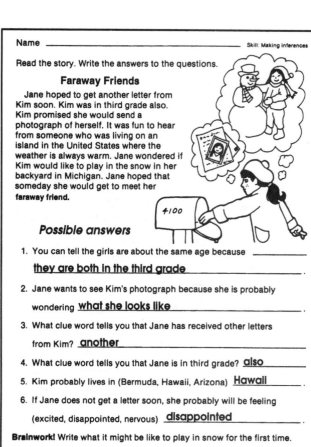

Possible answers

1. You can tell the girls are about the same age because **they are both in the third grade**

2. Jane wants to see Kim's photograph because she is probably wondering **what she looks like**

3. What clue word tells you that Jane has received other letters from Kim? **another**

4. What clue word tells you that Jane is in third grade? **also**

5. Kim probably lives in (Bermuda, Hawaii, Arizona) **Hawaii**

6. If Jane does not get a letter soon, she probably will be feeling (excited, disappointed, nervous) **disappointed**

Brainwork! Write what it might be like to play in snow for the first time.

Page 12

107

FS-32028 Critical Thinking

Answer Key

Page 13

Read the story and the two sentences after the story. Write the **true** sentence on the line.

1. The air is warm. Birds are singing in the morning. The grass is growing again. Flowers are starting to pop out of the ground. Soon days will be much longer.
   a. Spring is here.
   b. It is a hot summer day.

   Spring is here.

2. It was a special day in October. Beth made a jack-o-lantern. She put on her costume and carried a big bag. Then her mother took her to different houses. When she came home, she had candy in her bag.
   a. Beth went to a Halloween party.
   b. Beth went trick or treating.

   Beth went trick or treating.

3. Matt used a crayon to write his name on the bag. He made a peanut-butter-and-jelly sandwich and put it in the bag. He put in an apple and three cookies. Then he folded the top of the bag.
   a. Matt is hungry.
   b. Matt is packing his lunch.

   Matt is packing his lunch.

4. Sara telephoned her friend. She told her what happened at school that day. She said she hoped she would be at school tomorrow.
   a. Sara's friend moved away.
   b. Her friend was absent.

   Her friend was absent.

Brainwork! Draw a picture of one of the sentences that was false on this page.

Page 14

Read the story. Write a word from the Word Box to complete each sentence.

Word Box
tiny   brave
hungry   shy
frightened

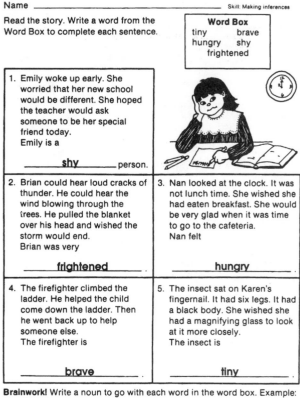

1. Emily woke up early. She worried that her new school would be different. She hoped the teacher would ask someone to be her special friend today.
   Emily is a _____**shy**_____ person.

2. Brian could hear loud cracks of thunder. He could hear the wind blowing through the trees. He pulled the blanket over his head and wished the storm would end.
   Brian was very
   _____**frightened**_____

3. Nan looked at the clock. It was not lunch time. She wished she had eaten breakfast. She would be very glad when it was time to go to the cafeteria.
   Nan felt
   _____**hungry**_____

4. The firefighter climbed the ladder. He helped the child come down the ladder. Then he went back up to help someone else.
   The firefighter is
   _____**brave**_____

5. The insect sat on Karen's fingernail. It had six legs. It had a black body. She wished she had a magnifying glass to look at it more closely.
   The insect is
   _____**tiny**_____

Brainwork! Write a noun to go with each word in the word box. Example: tiny (kitten)

Page 15

Read each story. Write a sentence to answer each question.
Possible answers

1. The dog ran inside the doghouse. He barked when he heard the thunder. He yelped when he saw the lightning in the sky. He curled up in the back corner of the doghouse.

   How was the dog feeling?
   The dog was feeling frightened.

2. Kate looked at her watch. She grabbed her sweater and her books. She hurried out the door. She ran to the corner where the school bus stopped.

   What time of day was it?
   It was morning.

3. Brent raised his hand. He showed the broken pencil point to the teacher. She told Brent that he could get up from his seat. He walked across the room. He took his pencil with him.

   Why did Brent raise his hand?
   Brent wanted to sharpen his pencil.

4. Mother fed the baby. Then she put the baby in her crib. She covered the baby with a blanket. She closed the curtains. Then she quietly walked out of the room.

   Why did mother need to close the curtains?
   Mother wanted the baby to take a nap.

Brainwork! Draw a picture of a girl playing in the snow. Write five sentences to describe your picture.

Page 16

Read the story. Follow the directions below each story. Do your BEST!!

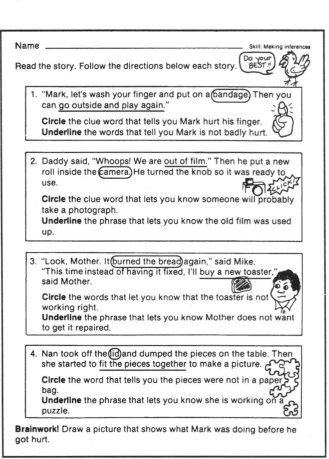

1. "Mark, let's wash your finger and put on a (bandage.) Then you can <u>go outside and play again.</u>"

   Circle the clue word that tells you Mark hurt his finger.
   Underline the words that tell you Mark is not badly hurt.

2. Daddy said, "Whoops! We are <u>out of film.</u>" Then he put a new roll inside the (camera.) He turned the knob so it was ready to use.

   Circle the clue word that lets you know someone will probably take a photograph.
   Underline the phrase that lets you know the old film was used up.

3. "Look, Mother. It (burned the bread) again," said Mike. "This time instead of having it fixed, <u>I'll buy a new toaster,</u>" said Mother.

   Circle the words that let you know that the toaster is not working right.
   Underline the phrase that lets you know Mother does not want to get it repaired.

4. Nan took off the (lid) and dumped the pieces on the table. Then she started to <u>fit the pieces together</u> to make a picture.

   Circle the word that tells you the pieces were not in a paper bag.
   Underline the phrase that lets you know she is working on a puzzle.

Brainwork! Draw a picture that shows what Mark was doing before he got hurt.

FS-32028 Critical Thinking

Answer Key

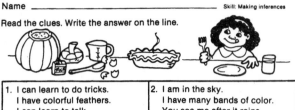

Making inferences

How Did They Know?

In the stories below, Dad and Mom each seem to know something without being told. How do they know? Read each story carefully. Think about the answer choices. On the lines, write the sentence that tells how they know.

Power Out!

Mom came home from work late one night. Everyone was asleep. When she tried to turn on the living room light, nothing happened. Then she tried the kitchen light. Finally, she lit a candle and looked at the clock. "The power must have gone out at 10:43," she said.

[10:43]

Mom knew exactly what time the power went off. How did she know?

- She came home after 10:43.
- The kitchen light didn't work.
- The clock had stopped at 10:43.

1. **The clock had stopped at 10:43.**

Long Gone?

Dad looked around the kitchen. He spied some cookie crumbs on a napkin and on the counter a glass of ice with a few drops of lemonade left in it. There was a note on the table that said, "I am going to Manny's for a couple of hours. Love, Nick."

Dad knew Nick hadn't been gone long. How did he know?

- The note said what time he left.
- The ice in the glass hadn't melted.
- Nick had eaten a cookie.

2. **The ice in the glass hadn't melted.**

Try This! Nick went to Manny's. Write three things you think *Manny's* could mean.

Page 17

Skill: Making inferences

Read the clues. Write the answer on the line.

1. I can learn to do tricks.
   I have colorful feathers.
   I can learn to talk.
   What am I?

   a parrot

   a puppet, a parrot, a puppy

2. I am in the sky.
   I have many bands of color.
   You see me after it rains.
   What am I?

   a rainbow

   the sun, a cloud, a rainbow

3. Use me to make a pie or carve a face on me.
   Roast and eat my seeds.
   What am I?

   a pumpkin

   an apple, a pumpkin, a cherry

4. I list words in ABC order.
   I can help you find out what a word means.
   What am I?

   a dictionary

   a dictionary, a storybook, a magazine

5. I have letters and numbers.
   I have a bell.
   Use me to talk to people.
   What am I?

   a telephone

   a letter, a telephone, a post card

6. You can read me everyday.
   I tell about the weather and what just happened.
   What am I?

   a newspaper

   a book, a story, a newspaper

Brainwork! Write clues about a person. Ask a friend to guess who it is.

Page 18

Skill: Making inferences

Read the story. Follow the directions below each story.

You can do it!

1. She put on her costume and mask. "My princess costume is beautiful. I'm so glad my mother knows how to (sew)" Ann said.

   Circle the word that tells you that Ann's mother probably made her costume.
   Underline the words that make you think she is going to a Halloween party.

2. Rick led the horse out of the barn. He put the (saddle) on the horse. He remembered looking at the colt when it was born. Now it was big and strong. (Neigh-h-h-h!)

   Circle the word that makes you think Rick will ride the horse.
   Underline the words that let you know Rick saw the colt when it was not big and strong.

3. Jay used the shovel to dig. The soil got soft. Then he opened the package of seeds. "Mother loves the way these (taste) so I hope these grow," Jay thought.

   Circle the word that tells you Jay is planting something you can eat.
   Underline the words that tell you the soil was hard.

4. The teacher asked a student to close the curtains. He asked another student to turn off the lights. The room got quiet. He turned on the (projector)

   Circle the word that tells you they are going to see a film.
   Underline the words that tell you the room had been noisy.

Brainwork! Draw four kinds of plants Jay might be planting.

Page 19

Skill: Making inferences

Read the story. Read the two sentences after the story. Write the **true** sentence on the line.

1. Sam crossed his fingers. Then he opened his mouth. The dentist looked at Sam's teeth. He told Sam he was doing a good job caring for his teeth.
   a. Sam has too many cavities.
   b. Sam has no cavities.

   Sam has no cavities.

2. There were leaves all over the ground. Amy helped her mother rake the leaves into big piles. Amy took the lid off the big trash can.
   a. They put the leaves in the can.
   b. They spread the leaves across the grass.

   They put the leaves in the can.

3. Daddy filled the tub with warm water. He opened the bottle of special shampoo. Then he picked up the dog and put him in the water.
   a. The dog is learning to swim.
   b. The dog is getting a bath.

   The dog is getting a bath.

4. Joe spread the icing on the cake. He put eight candles on the top. Then he told everyone to look at the fancy cake.
   a. It is someone's birthday.
   b. Dinner is ready now.

   It is someone's birthday.

Brainwork! Draw a picture of the cake Joe might make next year.

Page 20

Answer Key

Page 21

Name _____ Skill: Making Inferences

Read the story. Write a word from the Word Box to complete each sentence.

Word Box
surprised   windy
cranky   farm
proud

1. Sam fed the chickens. Then he let the cows out of the barn. After school he would take a ride on his horse. Sam lives on a

   __farm__

2. Pat hurried home from school. He pulled the paper out of his folder. He wanted to show Mother the big gold star on his spelling test. Pat is

   __proud__ of himself.

3. "This is the kind of day I have been waiting for," said Amy. "It is just perfect for my new kite. This is the biggest kite I have ever flown." It is a

   __windy__ day.

4. "Wow! This is great!" said Mike. "Even though it is my birthday, I didn't know there would be a party!" Mike is

   __surprised__

5. The baby didn't want to eat. He cried when his mother picked him up. Then he cried when she put him down. His mother said she didn't know what was wrong. The baby is

   __cranky__

Brainwork! Draw three faces to illustrate the three words that describe feelings in the Word Box. Write the word under each face.

Page 21

Page 22

Name _____ Inference

Read Between the Lines

If you read carefully, you can often learn information that is not actually stated. For example, if you read that Maria brought home her report card, you would know that Maria goes to school.

Read each story below. Circle **yes** or **no** after each statement.

1. Marci and Tom are twins. They are each on a soccer team. Marci's team has won one more game than Tom's team.
   a. Marci and Tom are on the same team. yes (no)
   b. Marci and Tom have the same mother. (yes) no

2. Daryl and Les are going to Cub Scout camp 20 miles from their school. Daryl's sister will drive them there.
   a. Daryl's sister is younger than Daryl. yes (no)
   b. Daryl and Les are boys. (yes) no

3. Carl is happy that his birthday is on Halloween. Ten months ago, on his seventh birthday, he had a big trick-or-treat party.
   a. Carl's birthday is on October 31. (yes) no
   b. Carl will turn eight on his next birthday. (yes) no

4. Jean has only two cousins. Both are sons of her Uncle Will and his wife Anne. Uncle Will is Jean's mother's brother.
   a. Jean's cousins are boys. (yes) no
   b. Will and Anne have no daughters. (yes) no

Try This! Dianne and Betsy have the same mother and father. Dianne's birthday is March 18. Betsy is exactly one year younger than Dianne. Write two more things you know about them.

Page 22

Page 23

Name _____ Skill: Making Inferences

Read each story. Write a sentence that answers each question.
Possible answers

1. Grandpa picked up the sewing box. He found a needle and thread. Then he picked up the shirt and the button.

   Why did Grandpa need a needle, thread and a button?

   __Grandpa wanted to sew on a button.__

2. Amy opened the cupboard. She got out the bag of food. Then she put the food in the dish and called the puppy.

   How can you tell that the puppy knows his name?

   __Amy called the puppy by name.__

3. The babysitter asked the twins to sit beside her. She opened the book. Then she told the twins she wanted them to take turns turning the pages. She told them she wanted them to listen.

   How do you know that the twins are not babies?

   __The twins knew how to turn pages.__

4. The children could see the smoke from the locomotive. The train was coming closer and closer. When the train got very close, they covered their ears.

   Why did the children cover their ears?

   __The train was loud.__

Brainwork! Would you like to be a twin? Why or why not?

Page 23

Page 24

Name _____ Making inferences

Read Between the Lines

Read each story carefully. Then follow the directions below it.
Possible answers
Marie Helps Herself

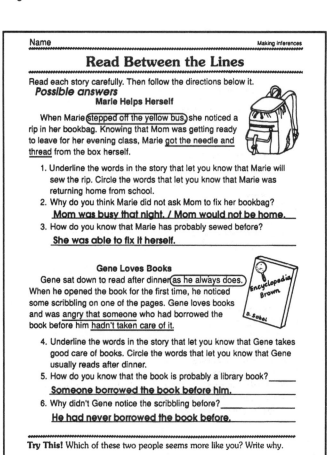

When Marie (stepped off the yellow bus,) she noticed a rip in her bookbag. Knowing that Mom was getting ready to leave for her evening class, Marie got the needle and thread from the box herself.

1. Underline the words in the story that let you know that Marie will sew the rip. Circle the words that let you know that Marie was returning home from school.
2. Why do you think Marie did not ask Mom to fix her bookbag?
   __Mom was busy that night. / Mom would not be home.__
3. How do you know that Marie has probably sewed before?
   __She was able to fix it herself.__

Gene Loves Books

Gene sat down to read after dinner (as he always does.) When he opened the book for the first time, he noticed some scribbling on one of the pages. Gene loves books and was angry that someone who had borrowed the book before him hadn't taken care of it.

4. Underline the words in the story that let you know that Gene takes good care of books. Circle the words that let you know that Gene usually reads after dinner.
5. How do you know that the book is probably a library book?
   __Someone borrowed the book before him.__
6. Why didn't Gene notice the scribbling before?
   __He had never borrowed the book before.__

Try This! Which of these two people seems more like you? Write why.

Page 24

Answer Key

      Skill: Making inferences

Read the clues. Write the answer on the line.

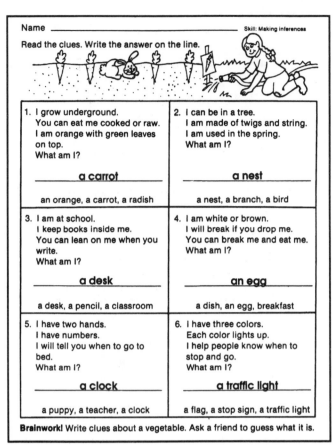

1. I grow underground.
   You can eat me cooked or raw.
   I am orange with green leaves on top.
   What am I?

   a carrot

   an orange, a carrot, a radish

2. I can be in a tree.
   I am made of twigs and string.
   I am used in the spring.
   What am I?

   a nest

   a nest, a branch, a bird

3. I am at school.
   I keep books inside me.
   You can lean on me when you write.
   What am I?

   a desk

   a desk, a pencil, a classroom

4. I am white or brown.
   I will break if you drop me.
   You can break me and eat me.
   What am I?

   an egg

   a dish, an egg, breakfast

5. I have two hands.
   I have numbers.
   I will tell you when to go to bed.
   What am I?

   a clock

   a puppy, a teacher, a clock

6. I have three colors.
   Each color lights up.
   I help people know when to stop and go.
   What am I?

   a traffic light

   a flag, a stop sign, a traffic light

Brainwork! Write clues about a vegetable. Ask a friend to guess what it is.

Page 25

      Skill: Making inferences

Read each story. Write a sentence that answers each question. *THINK!*

Possible answers

1. Mike saw some shiny objects on the floor. He picked them up. They were two quarters and one dime. He gave the money to his teacher. He told her where he found them.

   What kind of a person is Mike?

   Mike is an honest person.

2. Sara felt tired. She did not want to get out of bed. She did not want to play or eat. She didn't want to watch her favorite show on television.

   What could be wrong with Sara?

   Sara could be sick.

3. Dan looked at the puppies. He picked up the brown one. Then he held the black one. Dan could not decide which puppy he liked best.

   How was Dan feeling?

   Dan was feeling confused.

4. The teacher said, "You have all turned in your homework this week. You have earned an extra play period."

   Who is the teacher talking to?

   The teacher is talking to the class.

Brainwork! Draw a picture showing where Dan was as he looked at the puppies.

Page 26

      Making inferences

Bobby's Ride

Read the story about Bobby. Follow the directions below each part.

Possible answers

Part A

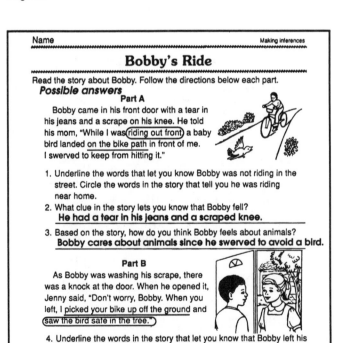

Bobby came in his front door with a tear in his jeans and a scrape on his knee. He told his mom, "While I was (riding out front) a baby bird landed on the bike path in front of me. I swerved to keep from hitting it."

1. Underline the words that let you know Bobby was not riding in the street. Circle the words in the story that tell you he was riding near home.
2. What clue in the story lets you know that Bobby fell?
   He had a tear in his jeans and a scraped knee.
3. Based on the story, how do you think Bobby feels about animals?
   Bobby cares about animals since he swerved to avoid a bird.

Part B

As Bobby was washing his scrape, there was a knock at the door. When he opened it, Jenny said, "Don't worry, Bobby. When you left, I picked your bike up off the ground and (saw the bird safe in the tree.")

4. Underline the words in the story that let you know that Bobby left his bike lying on the path. Circle the words that let you know that Jenny knew why Bobby swerved.
5. How can you tell that Jenny was near Bobby when the accident happened? **She came to the door while he was washing up.**
6. How can you tell that Bobby rushed right home after he fell?
   Bobby left his bike lying on the ground.

Try This! Based on the story, describe the kind of friend Jenny is.

Page 27

      Skill: Making inferences

Read the story. Write the answers to the questions.

Camp Sky High

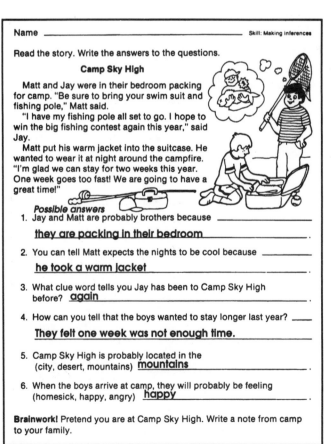

Matt and Jay were in their bedroom packing for camp. "Be sure to bring your swim suit and fishing pole," Matt said.

"I have my fishing pole all set to go. I hope to win the big fishing contest again this year," said Jay.

Matt put his warm jacket into the suitcase. He wanted to wear it at night around the campfire. "I'm glad we can stay for two weeks this year. One week goes too fast! We are going to have a great time!"

Possible answers

1. Jay and Matt are probably brothers because _____

   they are packing in their bedroom

2. You can tell Matt expects the nights to be cool because _____

   he took a warm jacket

3. What clue word tells you Jay has been to Camp Sky High before? **again**

4. How can you tell that the boys wanted to stay longer last year? _____

   They felt one week was not enough time.

5. Camp Sky High is probably located in the (city, desert, mountains) **mountains**

6. When the boys arrive at camp, they will probably be feeling (homesick, happy, angry) **happy**

Brainwork! Pretend you are at Camp Sky High. Write a note from camp to your family.

Page 28

Answer Key

Read the story. Write the answers to the questions.

Very Special Visitors

For a birthday treat, Dan's mother was taking him to the zoo. He could invite a friend to go, too. "The newspaper says that they will only be there for one more month," Mother said.

"I have always wanted to see real pandas. They look so cute in pictures. I hope they are as much fun to watch as the monkeys," said Danny. "I know Chris will like the zoo because he reads books about animals."

1. You can tell there is a newspaper article about pandas in the zoo because **Mother read about it**

2. How do you think Chris feels about animals? **He likes them**

3. How can you tell Danny has been to a zoo before? **He has seen the monkeys**

4. Danny probably knows what pandas look like because **He has seen pictures in books**

5. How can you tell the pandas are not always at the zoo? **They will be at the zoo for one more month**

6. Chris is Danny's (brother, cousin, friend) **friend**

Brainwork! Choose an animal you think is cute. Write five words to describe it.

Snowball's Escape

Jason got the hamster food from the shelf and walked toward Snowball's cage. But Snowball was not in sight. He was not on his running wheel or asleep under his bedding. There was nowhere else in the cage Snowball could be hiding!

At first Jason wondered how Snowball could have escaped. Then he realized that the cage cover was leaning against his bed. Jason felt guilty since he was the only one who took care of Snowball.

Suddenly Jason heard a sound from inside the closet next to the cage. When he opened the door, there was Snowball curled up in Jason's sneaker!

1. What kind of animal is Snowball? **hamster** How do you know? **Jason got hamster food.**

2. Is Snowball male or female? **male** How do you know? **The story uses "he" when talking about Snowball.**

3. How was Snowball able to escape? **The cover was not on the cage.**

4. Why did Jason feel guilty? **Jason believed that he had forgotten to cover the cage.**

5. In what room was Snowball's cage? **Jason's bedroom** How do you know? **The cover was leaning against his bed.**

Try This! Write why you think Snowball crawled into Jason's sneaker.

Circle the right answers for each question.

1. What do you do in math?
   (add) (divide) swim (multiply) (subtract)

2. Which jewels could be used to make a ring?
   (ruby) (jade) (diamond) (emerald) apple

3. Which ones are snakes?
   (cobra) hawk (boa) (garter) (copperhead)

4. Which ones are baby animals?
   dog (colt) (cub) (calf) (kitten)

5. Which ones are planets?
   (Mars) (Venus) (Jupiter) Texas (Earth)

6. Which ones are made of water?
   (ocean) (ice) (puddle) (stream) hill

7. Which ones give off light?
   (sun) desk (fire) (lamp) (torch)

8. What would you find on a kitchen table?
   (salt) (plate) barn (knife) (napkin)

9. Which ones tell how something feels?
   (hard) (sharp) lemon (sticky) (soft)

10. Which ones are round?
    (ball) (donut) (penny) box (bubble)

11. Which ones have two legs?
    (chicken) (person) (bird) (duck) cow

12. What would you see in a garden?
    desk (corn) (scarecrow) (hoe) (carrots)

Write each word from the word box under the right category.
Order of answers may vary.

1. Sounds	2. U.S. States	3. Body Parts
fizz	Ohio	skin
hoot	Texas	ribs
howl	Maine	lungs
growl	Kansas	heart
laugh	Hawaii	bones
squeak	Alaska	blood
whisper	New York	muscles

Word Box

skin	hoot	Texas	laugh	bones	Hawaii	muscles
fizz	ribs	lungs	Maine	blood	squeak	whisper
Ohio	howl	growl	heart	Kansas	Alaska	New York

FS-32028 Critical Thinking

Answer Key

Page 33

Name _____ Skill: Categorization

Mind Teasers

Write what each group
of words has in common.

Possible answers

1. piggy bank   purse   savings   cash register

   places to put money

2. bench   stool   sofa   chair

   things to sit on

3. nurse   milkman   doctor   maid

   occupations

4. read   blink   stare   cross

   things your eyes do

5. penguin   zebra   panda bear   newspaper

   black and white things

6. hiss   giggle   snore   creak

   sounds

7. Eskimo   igloo   polar bear   icebergs

   things found in Alaska

8. stable   saddle   harness   gallop

   things identified with a horse

9. Red Rover   Handball   Tag   Dodgeball

   playground games

10. coat   blanket   fire   mittens

   things to keep you warm

Page 33

Page 34

Name _____ Skill: Categorization

Write the name of the category at the **top** of each box.
Then write two more things that belong to each category.

Possible categories

1. Baby Things	2. Family
bottle	Dad
crib	sister
diaper	Mom
answers	*answers*
vary	*vary*

3. Rhyming Words	4. Trees	5. Car Parts
cake	pine	tires
lake	maple	brake
bake	oak	engine
answers	*answers*	*answers*
vary	*vary*	*vary*

6. Breakfast	7. Hot Things	8. Homes
bacon	heater	igloo
cereal	iron	castle
eggs	coffee pot	apartment
answers	*answers*	*answers*
vary	*vary*	*vary*

Page 34

Page 35

Name _____ Skill: Categorization

Write a word for each category that
starts with the letter given.

Answers vary

	Animals	Transportation	Jobs
T			
S			
C			
A			

T S C A B S H T

	Names of Girls	Sports	Food
B			
S			
H			
T			

Page 35

Page 36

Name _____ *Order of answers may vary.* Skill: Categorization

Write each word from the word box under the right category.

1. Feelings	2. Sports	3. Materials
sick	golf	wood
sad	boxing	cloth
angry	tennis	steel
happy	hockey	glass
brave	swimming	brass
scared	baseball	rubber
excited	football	plastic

Word Box

sick	golf	steel	brass	boxing	excited	swimming
wood	cloth	glass	brave	tennis	hockey	baseball
sad	angry	happy	scared	rubber	plastic	football

Page 36

113

FS-32028 Critical Thinking

Answer Key

Page 37

Circle the right answers for each question.

1. Which ones are jobs?
   (nurse)   (barber)   (pilot)   (carpenter)   puppy

2. Which ones are parts of a house?
   grass   (door)   (window)   (wall)   (roof)

3. What would you find in a forest?
   (trees)   whale   (chipmunk)   (pine cones)   (deer)

4. Which ones are time words?
   (day)   (year)   penny   (month)   (week)

5. Which ones are trees?
   (pine)   (elm)   (oak)   daisy   (spruce)

6. Which ones live in the ocean?
   (seal)   pig   (shark)   (octopus)   (whale)

7. Which ones are countries?
   (Japan)   (U.S.A.)   (Canada)   Kansas   (Mexico)

8. Which ones are directions?
   far   (north)   (east)   (south)   (west)

9. In which ones could you ride?
   (car)   (truck)   (wagon)   (boat)   stove

10. Which ones are too heavy to carry?
    (elephant)   feather   (house)   (car)   (cow)

11. Which ones can you wear?
    (pants)   (coat)   (shirt)   lamp   (shoes)

12. Which ones measure something?
    (ruler)   (teaspoon)   purse   (cup)   (yardstick)

Page 37

Page 38

Write the name of the category at the top of each box.
Then write two more things that belong to each category.

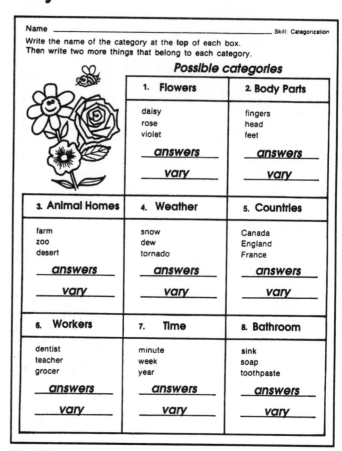

Possible categories

1. Flowers	2. Body Parts
daisy	fingers
rose	head
violet	feet
answers	*answers*
vary	*vary*

3. Animal Homes	4. Weather	5. Countries
farm	snow	Canada
zoo	dew	England
desert	tornado	France
answers	*answers*	*answers*
vary	*vary*	*vary*

6. Workers	7. Time	8. Bathroom
dentist	minute	sink
teacher	week	soap
grocer	year	toothpaste
answers	*answers*	*answers*
vary	*vary*	*vary*

Page 38

Page 39

Write the name of the holiday for each picture.
The answers are in the pot of gold.

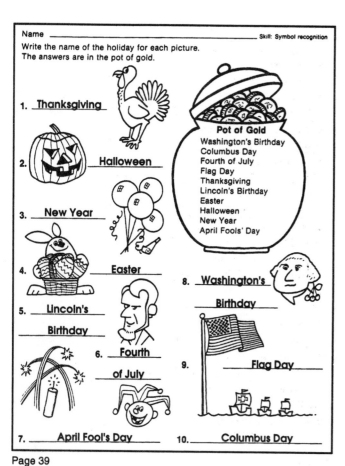

Pot of Gold
Washington's Birthday
Columbus Day
Fourth of July
Flag Day
Thanksgiving
Lincoln's Birthday
Easter
Halloween
New Year
April Fools' Day

1. Thanksgiving
2. Halloween
3. New Year
4. Easter
5. Lincoln's Birthday
6. Fourth of July
7. April Fool's Day
8. Washington's Birthday
9. Flag Day
10. Columbus Day

Page 39

Page 40

Mind Teasers

Write what each group of words has in common.

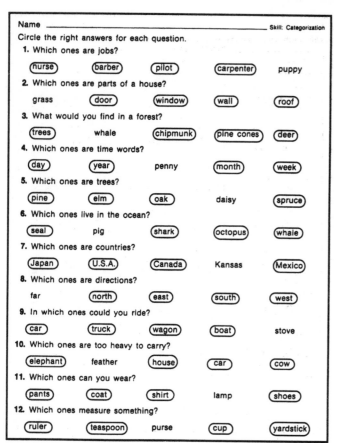

Possible answers

1. horseshoe   four-leaf clover   number seven
   lucky things

2. window   mirror   vase   crystal ball
   things made of glass

3. rabbit   marshmallow   pillow   cotton
   soft things

4. whizz   quiz   Liz   fizz
   words that rhyme

5. sled   snowshoes   skis   toboggan
   things to use in the snow

6. sailboat   kite   windmill   pinwheel
   things that need wind

7. unicorn   dragon   troll   leprechaun
   make-believe characters

8. math   reading   science   music
   school subjects

9. bitter   sweet   sour   salty
   how things taste

10. runway   airplane   control tower   tickets
    things at an airport

Page 40

Answer Key

FS-32028 Critical Thinking

Name _____ Skill: Categorization

Write the name of the category at the **top** of each box.
Then write two more things that belong to each category.

Possible categories

1. **Bread**	2. **Sports**	3. **Water Travel**
white	surfing	sailboat
rye	ice skating	raft
whole wheat	basketball	canoe
Answers	_Answers_	_Answers_
vary	_vary_	_vary_

4. **States**	5. **Fruits**	6. **Planets**
Maryland	apples	Saturn
Alabama	oranges	Neptune
Kentucky	plums	Pluto
Answers	_Answers_	_Answers_
vary	_vary_	_vary_

7. **Musical Instruments**	8. **Dogs**	
piano	poodle	
violin	cocker spaniel	
flute	collie	
Answers	_Answers_	
vary	_vary_	

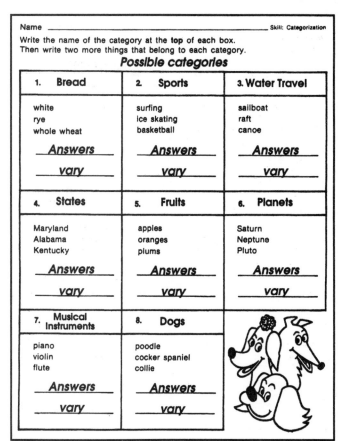

Page 41

Name _____ Skill: Categorization

Write each word from the word box under the right category.
Order of Answers may vary.

1. Classroom	2. Birthday Things	3. Musical Instruments
chalk	cake	harp
desks	candy	tuba
paints	gifts	drums
erasers	suckers	flute
pencils	candles	piano
paper	nut cups	guitar
scissors	ice cream	cymbals

Word Box

cake	drums	desks	piano	suckers	cymbals	scissors
harp	candy	gifts	paints	erasers	paper	nut cups
tuba	chalk	flute	guitar	pencils	candles	ice cream

Page 42

Name _____ Skill: Categorization

Possible answers   **Mind Teasers**

Write what each group
of words has in common.

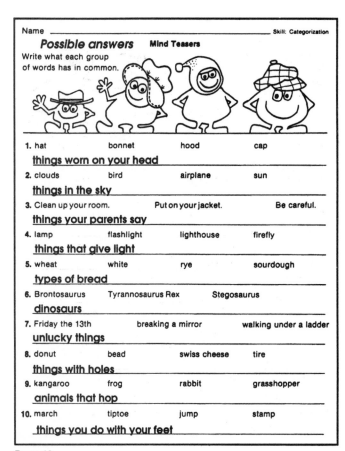

1. hat   bonnet   hood   cap
   __things worn on your head__
2. clouds   bird   airplane   sun
   __things in the sky__
3. Clean up your room.   Put on your jacket.   Be careful.
   __things your parents say__
4. lamp   flashlight   lighthouse   firefly
   __things that give light__
5. wheat   white   rye   sourdough
   __types of bread__
6. Brontosaurus   Tyrannosaurus Rex   Stegosaurus
   __dinosaurs__
7. Friday the 13th   breaking a mirror   walking under a ladder
   __unlucky things__
8. donut   bead   swiss cheese   tire
   __things with holes__
9. kangaroo   frog   rabbit   grasshopper
   __animals that hop__
10. march   tiptoe   jump   stamp
    __things you do with your feet__

Page 43

Name _____ Skill: Categorization

Circle the right answers for each question.
1. Which ones are birds?
   monkey   (crow)   (owl)   (parrot)   (dove)
2. Which ones are easy to lift?
   (pillow)   car   (pencil)   (spoon)   (comb)
3. What would you need to go camping?
   (tent)   (sleeping bag)   cat   (flashlight)   (compass)
4. What would you find in a living room?
   (TV)   (couch)   (table)   bathtub   (lamp)
5. Which ones are your relatives?
   (uncle)   (grandpa)   (aunt)   (cousin)   teacher
6. Which sports do not need a ball?
   (hockey)   ping pong   (skating)   (diving)   (skiing)
7. What could you use in the rain?
   trunks   (umbrella)   (boots)   (coat)   (hood)
8. Which ones are tools?
   (saw)   (shovel)   (ax)   (hammer)   pants
9. Which ones are made out of cloth?
   (dress)   (curtains)   (shirt)   stove   (bedspread)
10. Who works at a school?
    florist   (principal)   (teacher)   (custodian)   (secretary)
11. Which ones can be found in the air?
    (helicopter)   (jet)   train   (blimp)   (glider)
12. Which ones are names for boys?
    (Adam)   (Scott)   (Mark)   (Brad)   Holly

Page 44

115

FS-32028 Critical Thinking

Answer Key

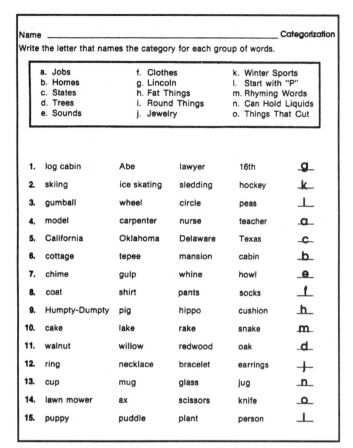

Name _____ Categorization

Write the letter that names the category for each group of words.

a. Jobs	f. Clothes	k. Winter Sports
b. Homes	g. Lincoln	l. Start with "P"
c. States	h. Fat Things	m. Rhyming Words
d. Trees	i. Round Things	n. Can Hold Liquids
e. Sounds	j. Jewelry	o. Things That Cut

#					
1.	log cabin	Abe	lawyer	16th	g
2.	skiing	ice skating	sledding	hockey	k
3.	gumball	wheel	circle	peas	i
4.	model	carpenter	nurse	teacher	a
5.	California	Oklahoma	Delaware	Texas	c
6.	cottage	tepee	mansion	cabin	b
7.	chime	gulp	whine	howl	e
8.	coat	shirt	pants	socks	f
9.	Humpty-Dumpty	pig	hippo	cushion	h
10.	cake	lake	rake	snake	m
11.	walnut	willow	redwood	oak	d
12.	ring	necklace	bracelet	earrings	j
13.	cup	mug	glass	jug	n
14.	lawn mower	ax	scissors	knife	o
15.	puppy	puddle	plant	person	l

Page 45

Name _____ Skill: Classification

Write who or what goes with each story. The storybook will help you!

Prince
Three Bears
Magic Lamp
Seven Dwarfs
Captain Hook

Wolf
Tigger
Dorothy
Huck Finn
Giant

1. Goldilocks **Three Bears**
2. Cinderella **Prince**
3. Peter Pan **Captain Hook**
4. Three Little Pigs **Wolf**
5. Jack and the Beanstalk **Giant**
6. Wizard of Oz **Dorothy**
7. Winnie-the-Pooh **Tigger**
8. Tom Sawyer **Huck Finn**
9. Aladdin **Magic Lamp**
10. Snow White **Seven Dwarfs**

Page 46

Name _____ Analogies

As It Is

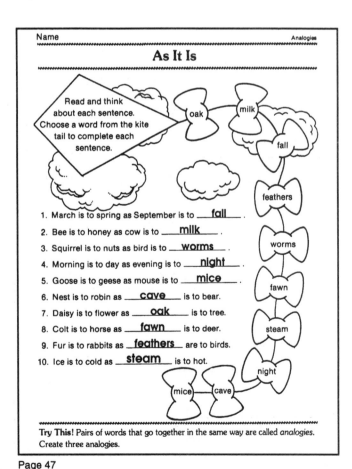

Read and think about each sentence. Choose a word from the kite tail to complete each sentence.

1. March is to spring as September is to ___fall___ .
2. Bee is to honey as cow is to ___milk___ .
3. Squirrel is to nuts as bird is to ___worms___ .
4. Morning is to day as evening is to ___night___ .
5. Goose is to geese as mouse is to ___mice___ .
6. Nest is to robin as ___cave___ is to bear.
7. Daisy is to flower as ___oak___ is to tree.
8. Colt is to horse as ___fawn___ is to deer.
9. Fur is to rabbits as ___feathers___ are to birds.
10. Ice is to cold as ___steam___ is to hot.

Try This! Pairs of words that go together in the same way are called *analogies*. Create three analogies.

Page 47

Name _____ Skill: Analogies

Each pair of words goes together in the same way. What is the relationship? Write each one on the line.

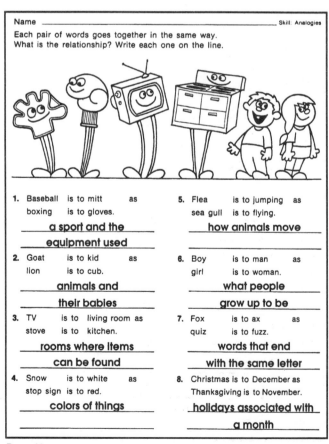

1. Baseball is to mitt as boxing is to gloves.
   ___a sport and the___
   ___equipment used___

2. Goat is to kid as lion is to cub.
   ___animals and___
   ___their babies___

3. TV is to living room as stove is to kitchen.
   ___rooms where items___
   ___can be found___

4. Snow is to white as stop sign is to red.
   ___colors of things___
   _____

5. Flea is to jumping as sea gull is to flying.
   ___how animals move___
   _____

6. Boy is to man as girl is to woman.
   ___what people___
   ___grow up to be___

7. Fox is to ax as quiz is to fuzz.
   ___words that end___
   ___with the same letter___

8. Christmas is to December as Thanksgiving is to November.
   ___holidays associated with___
   ___a month___

Page 48

FS-32028 Critical Thinking

Answer Key

Name _____   Skill: Analogies

Each pair of words goes together in the same way.
Write the missing word on the line. The word box will help you.

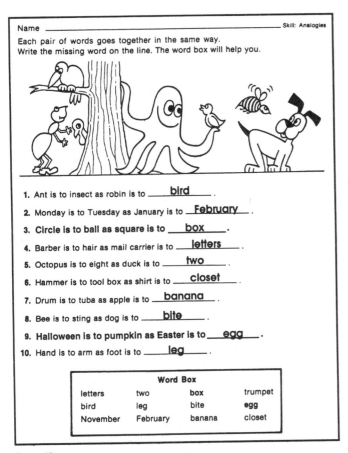

1. Ant is to insect as robin is to __bird__ .
2. Monday is to Tuesday as January is to __February__ .
3. Circle is to ball as square is to __box__ .
4. Barber is to hair as mail carrier is to __letters__ .
5. Octopus is to eight as duck is to __two__ .
6. Hammer is to tool box as shirt is to __closet__ .
7. Drum is to tuba as apple is to __banana__ .
8. Bee is to sting as dog is to __bite__ .
9. Halloween is to pumpkin as Easter is to __egg__ .
10. Hand is to arm as foot is to __leg__ .

Word Box			
letters	two	box	trumpet
bird	leg	bite	egg
November	February	banana	closet

Page 49

Name _____   Skill: Analogies

Each pair of words goes together in the same way.
Write the missing word on the line. The word box will help you.

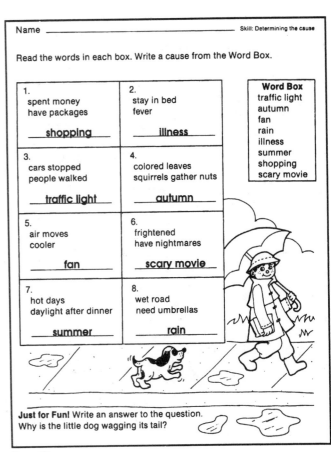

1. Tiger is to jungle as pig is to __farm__ .
2. Tent is to sleeping bag as house is to __bed__ .
3. State is to New York as country is to __France__ .
4. Water is to boat as land is to __train__ .
5. Carpenter is to hammer as gardener is to __hoe__ .
6. Swim is to water as fly is to __air__ .
7. Dog is to bark as duck is to __quack__ .
8. Touch is to fur as taste is to __pizza__ .
9. Lincoln is to sixteenth as Washington is to __first__ .
10. Pillow is to soft as rock is to __hard__ .

Word Box			
bed	France	hoe	hard
quack	farm	moo	first
pizza	air	water	train

Page 50

Name _____   Skill: Analogies

Each pair of words goes together in the same way.
Write the missing word on the line. The word box will help you.

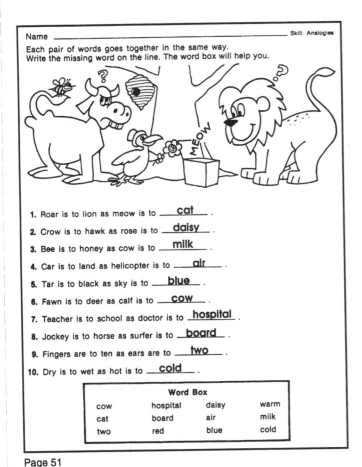

1. Roar is to lion as meow is to __cat__ .
2. Crow is to hawk as rose is to __daisy__ .
3. Bee is to honey as cow is to __milk__ .
4. Car is to land as helicopter is to __air__ .
5. Tar is to black as sky is to __blue__ .
6. Fawn is to deer as calf is to __cow__ .
7. Teacher is to school as doctor is to __hospital__ .
8. Jockey is to horse as surfer is to __board__ .
9. Fingers are to ten as ears are to __two__ .
10. Dry is to wet as hot is to __cold__ .

Word Box			
cow	hospital	daisy	warm
cat	board	air	milk
two	red	blue	cold

Page 51

Name _____   Skill: Determining the cause

Read the words in each box. Write a cause from the Word Box.

		Word Box
1. spent money have packages __shopping__	2. stay in bed fever __illness__	traffic light autumn fan rain illness summer shopping scary movie
3. cars stopped people walked __traffic light__	4. colored leaves squirrels gather nuts __autumn__	
5. air moves cooler __fan__	6. frightened have nightmares __scary movie__	
7. hot days daylight after dinner __summer__	8. wet road need umbrellas __rain__	

Just for Fun! Write an answer to the question.
Why is the little dog wagging its tail?

Page 52

FS-32028 Critical Thinking

Answer Key

Page 53

Name _____ Skill: Determining the cause

Read the words in each box. Write a cause from the Word Box.

1. turn on water pick up soap **wash hands**	2. get a pencil take out paper **write**
3. tent parade **circus**	4. tears frown **crying**
5. mix batter pans in oven **bake**	6. pack suitcase say goodbye **vacation**
7. take turns roll the dice **game**	8. take books take lunch **school**

Word Box
circus
vacation
write
game
crying
school
wash hands
bake

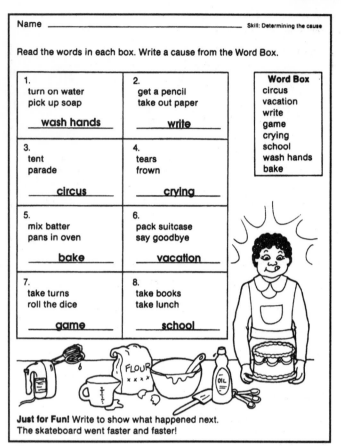

Just for Fun! Write to show what happened next.
The skateboard went faster and faster!

Page 53

Page 54

Name _____ Skill: Determining the cause

Read the words in each box. Write a cause from the Word Box.

1. put on bathing suit jump in water **want to swim**	2. put on coat open the door **will go out**
3. pick up receiver say hello **telephone rang**	4. get crayons get art paper **want to draw**
5. get a needle use some thread **want to sew**	6. look to right look to left **will cross a road**
7. lick a stamp seal the envelope **will mail a card**	8. say "ouch" finger bleeds **a cut**

Word Box
want to sew	a cut
will cross a road	want to draw
will go out	telephone rang
want to swim	will mail a card

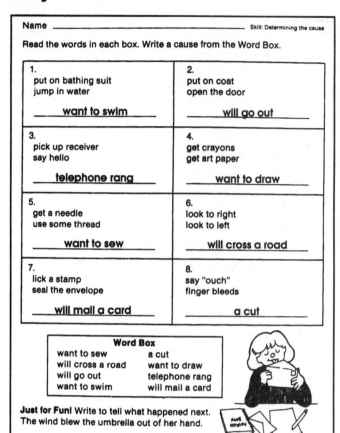

Just for Fun! Write to tell what happened next.
The wind blew the umbrella out of her hand.

Page 54

Page 55

Name _____ Skill: Determining the cause

Read the words in each box. Write a cause from the Word Box.

1. flames smoke **fire**	2. lost key lost coins **hole in pocket**
3. blowing leaves kites can fly **wind**	4. cold weather gets dark early **winter**
5. barking chewed shoe **puppy**	6. need a key will not open **locked**
7. dark bedtime **night**	8. cake candles **birthday**

Word Box
winter
locked
fire
hole in pocket
wind
puppy
birthday
night

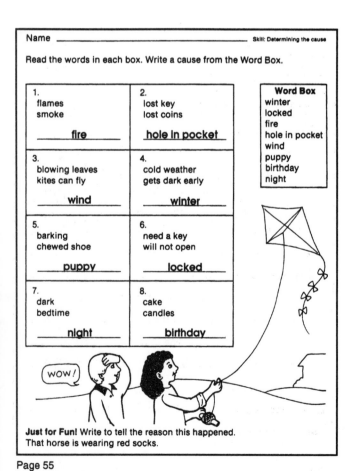

Just for Fun! Write to tell the reason this happened.
That horse is wearing red socks.

Page 55

Page 56

Name _____ Skill: Determining the cause

Read the words in each box. Write a cause from the Word Box.

1. puddles wet streets **rain**	2. dream rest **sleep**
3. cool days leaves fall **autumn**	4. flowers bloom birds build nests **spring**
5. tired out of breath **running**	6. wake up get dressed **morning**
7. chew swallow **eat**	8. no school time to play **weekend**

Word Box
sleep
eat
weekend
rain
morning
running
autumn
spring

Just for Fun! Write to tell the reason this happened.
The boy's picture was in the newspaper.

Page 56

118

FS-32028 Critical Thinking

Answer Key

Page 57

Name _____ Skill: Determining cause and effect

Write a word from the Word Box to complete each sentence.

Word Box

dark	grow	lost	fell
asleep	loud	dry	rang

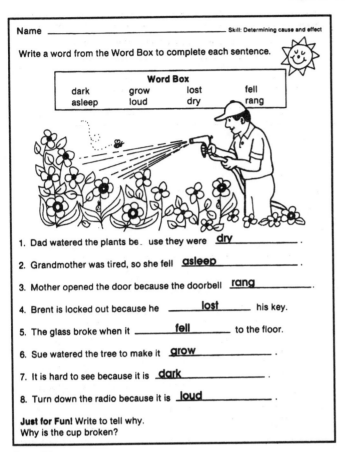

1. Dad watered the plants be_use they were __dry__ .

2. Grandmother was tired, so she fell __asleep__ .

3. Mother opened the door because the doorbell __rang__ .

4. Brent is locked out because he __lost__ his key.

5. The glass broke when it __fell__ to the floor.

6. Sue watered the tree to make it __grow__ .

7. It is hard to see because it is __dark__ .

8. Turn down the radio because it is __loud__ .

Just for Fun! Write to tell why.
Why is the cup broken?

Page 57

Page 58

Name _____ Skill: Determining cause and effect

Write a phrase from the Word Box to complete each sentence.

Word Box

cars would stop	would not tip
train was coming	gathered twigs
would see her	heard the sirens
she was cold	caught a fish

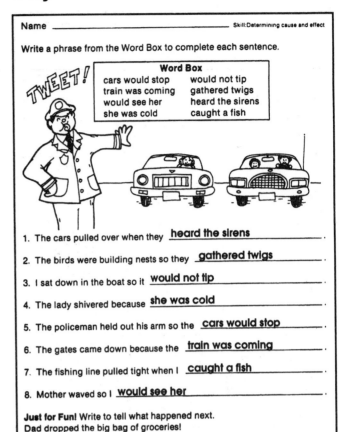

1. The cars pulled over when they __heard the sirens__ .

2. The birds were building nests so they __gathered twigs__ .

3. I sat down in the boat so it __would not tip__ .

4. The lady shivered because __she was cold__ .

5. The policeman held out his arm so the __cars would stop__ .

6. The gates came down because the __train was coming__ .

7. The fishing line pulled tight when I __caught a fish__ .

8. Mother waved so I __would see her__ .

Just for Fun! Write to tell what happened next.
Dad dropped the big bag of groceries!

Page 58

Page 59

Name _____ Skill: Determining cause and effect

Write a word from the Word Box to complete each sentence.

Word Box

party	funny	raining	wake
late	absent	colder	strong

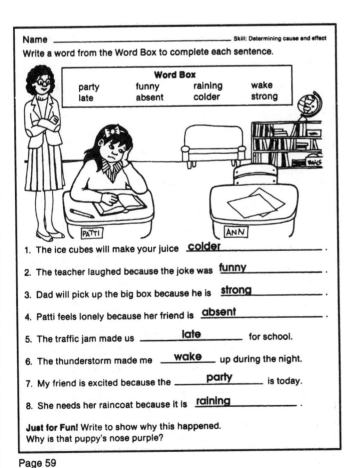

1. The ice cubes will make your juice __colder__ .

2. The teacher laughed because the joke was __funny__ .

3. Dad will pick up the big box because he is __strong__ .

4. Patti feels lonely because her friend is __absent__ .

5. The traffic jam made us __late__ for school.

6. The thunderstorm made me __wake__ up during the night.

7. My friend is excited because the __party__ is today.

8. She needs her raincoat because it is __raining__ .

Just for Fun! Write to show why this happened.
Why is that puppy's nose purple?

Page 59

Page 60

Name _____ Skill: Determining cause and effect

Write a phrase from the Word Box to complete each sentence.

Word Box

is a collector	it is wet
would look pretty	would stay out
know the number	bug bit her
would be straight	be safe

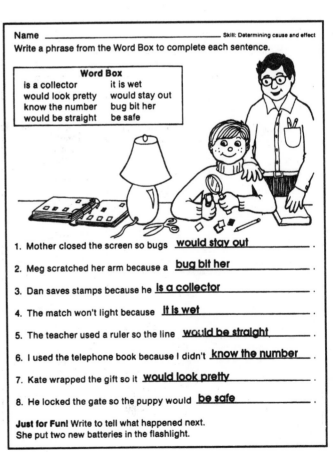

1. Mother closed the screen so bugs __would stay out__ .

2. Meg scratched her arm because a __bug bit her__ .

3. Dan saves stamps because he __is a collector__ .

4. The match won't light because __it is wet__ .

5. The teacher used a ruler so the line __would be straight__ .

6. I used the telephone book because I didn't __know the number__ .

7. Kate wrapped the gift so it __would look pretty__ .

8. He locked the gate so the puppy would __be safe__ .

Just for Fun! Write to tell what happened next.
She put two new batteries in the flashlight.

Page 60

FS-32028 Critical Thinking

Answer Key

Name

Skill: Determining cause and effect,
Completing sentences

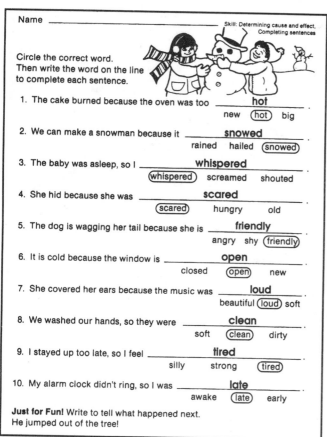

Circle the correct word.
Then write the word on the line
to complete each sentence.

1. The cake burned because the oven was too **hot**
   new (hot) big

2. We can make a snowman because it **snowed**
   rained hailed (snowed)

3. The baby was asleep, so I **whispered**
   (whispered) screamed shouted

4. She hid because she was **scared**
   (scared) hungry old

5. The dog is wagging her tail because she is **friendly**
   angry shy (friendly)

6. It is cold because the window is **open**
   closed (open) new

7. She covered her ears because the music was **loud**
   beautiful (loud) soft

8. We washed our hands, so they were **clean**
   soft (clean) dirty

9. I stayed up too late, so I feel **tired**
   silly strong (tired)

10. My alarm clock didn't ring, so I was **late**
    awake (late) early

Just for Fun! Write to tell what happened next.
He jumped out of the tree!

Page 61

Name

Skill: Determining cause and effect

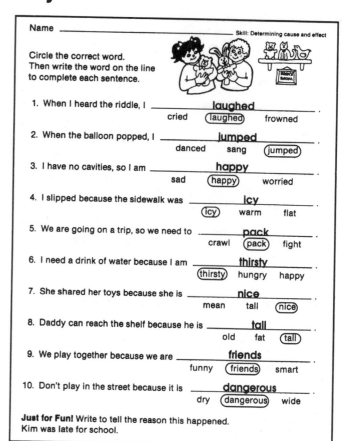

Circle the correct word.
Then write the word on the line
to complete each sentence.

1. When I heard the riddle, I **laughed**
   cried (laughed) frowned

2. When the balloon popped, I **jumped**
   danced sang (jumped)

3. I have no cavities, so I am **happy**
   sad (happy) worried

4. I slipped because the sidewalk was **icy**
   (icy) warm flat

5. We are going on a trip, so we need to **pack**
   crawl (pack) fight

6. I need a drink of water because I am **thirsty**
   (thirsty) hungry happy

7. She shared her toys because she is **nice**
   mean tall (nice)

8. Daddy can reach the shelf because he is **tall**
   old fat (tall)

9. We play together because we are **friends**
   funny (friends) smart

10. Don't play in the street because it is **dangerous**
    dry (dangerous) wide

Just for Fun! Write to tell the reason this happened.
Kim was late for school.

Page 62

Name

Skill: Determining cause and effect

Write a word from the Word Box to complete each sentence.

Word Box			
empty	wind	tight	hot
sugar	dirty	sneeze	save

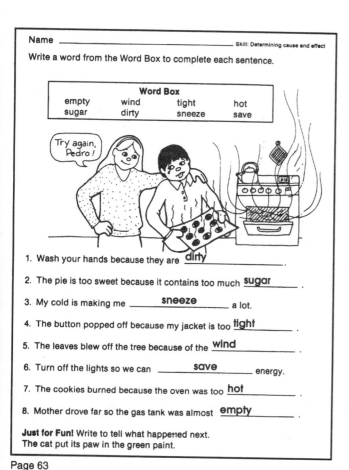

Try again, Pedro!

1. Wash your hands because they are **dirty**

2. The pie is too sweet because it contains too much **sugar**

3. My cold is making me **sneeze** a lot.

4. The button popped off because my jacket is too **tight**

5. The leaves blew off the tree because of the **wind**

6. Turn off the lights so we can **save** energy.

7. The cookies burned because the oven was too **hot**

8. Mother drove far so the gas tank was almost **empty**

Just for Fun! Write to tell what happened next.
The cat put its paw in the green paint.

Page 63

Name

Skill: Determining cause and effect

Write a phrase from the Word Box to complete each sentence.

Word Box	
ride her bike	has a leak
took the picture	touch the wall
hands were cold	it is dull
hungry before lunch	a new one

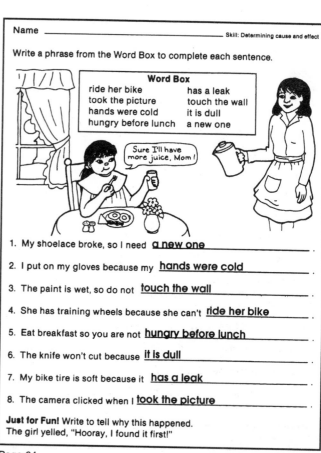

Sure I'll have more juice, Mom!

1. My shoelace broke, so I need **a new one**

2. I put on my gloves because my **hands were cold**

3. The paint is wet, so do not **touch the wall**

4. She has training wheels because she can't **ride her bike**

5. Eat breakfast so you are not **hungry before lunch**

6. The knife won't cut because **it is dull**

7. My bike tire is soft because it **has a leak**

8. The camera clicked when I **took the picture**

Just for Fun! Write to tell why this happened.
The girl yelled, "Hooray, I found it first!"

Page 64

FS-32028 Critical Thinking

Answer Key

Circle the correct word.
Then write the word on the line to complete each sentence.

1. I can't play because I am _____ **Ill** _____ .
   happy (ill) wise

2. There is no school because it is _____ **Sunday** _____ .
   sunny cloudy (Sunday)

3. When the scary ghost popped out, I _____ **screamed** _____ .
   relaxed (screamed) yawned

4. He won the race because he ran _____ **fast** _____ .
   quietly noisily (fast)

5. The squirrel gathers nuts because it will soon be _____ **winter** _____ .
   (winter) hot Friday

6. The people clapped because the show was _____ **good** _____ .
   (good) boring strange

7. Because the girls are sisters, they look _____ **alike** _____ .
   hot tired (alike)

8. We can plant the flowers because it is _____ **spring** _____ .
   snowing (spring) dark

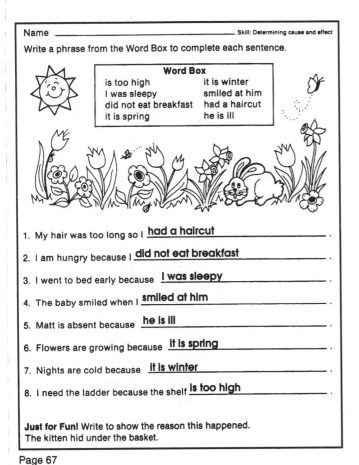

Just for Fun! Write to tell why this happened.
Everyone clapped and cheered!

Page 65

Write a word from the Word Box to complete each sentence.

Word Box
| brush | helping | tight | hungry |
| sticky | practice | warmer | birthday |

I hope you'll like this gift!

1. I can't open the jar because the lid is too **tight** _____ .
2. Turn on the heater so the room will get **warmer** _____ .
3. The paste makes my fingers **sticky** _____ .
4. She gave me a gift because it is my **birthday** _____ .
5. The smell of dinner cooking makes me feel **hungry** _____ .
6. Dad thanked me for _____ **helping** _____ with the dishes.
7. I play the piano better because I _____ **practice** _____ each day.
8. I have no cavities because I _____ **brush** _____ my teeth.

Just for Fun! Write to tell the reason this happened.
The frog jumped on the lily pad.

Page 66

Write a phrase from the Word Box to complete each sentence.

Word Box
is too high	it is winter
I was sleepy	smiled at him
did not eat breakfast	had a haircut
it is spring	he is ill

1. My hair was too long so I **had a haircut** _____ .
2. I am hungry because I **did not eat breakfast** _____ .
3. I went to bed early because **I was sleepy** _____ .
4. The baby smiled when I **smiled at him** _____ .
5. Matt is absent because **he is ill** _____ .
6. Flowers are growing because **it is spring** _____ .
7. Nights are cold because **it is winter** _____ .
8. I need the ladder because the shelf **is too high** _____ .

Just for Fun! Write to show the reason this happened.
The kitten hid under the basket.

Page 67

Circle the correct word.
Then write the word on the line to complete each sentence.

1. I studied because I want my score to be _____ **good** _____
   (good) neat hard

2. She takes turns because she is _____ **fair** _____
   old (fair) funny

3. My best friend is absent, so I am _____ **lonely** _____
   happy angry (lonely)

4. Mother is taking a nap because she is _____ **tired** _____
   (tired) silly relaxed

5. I cross in the crosswalk because it is _____ **safe** _____
   fun dangerous (safe)

6. My tooth is aching, so I will see the _____ **dentist** _____
   movie (dentist) vet

7. Dad worried because I was _____ **late** _____
   early friendly (late)

8. I like stuffed animals because they are _____ **cuddly** _____
   scary (cuddly) hard

9. My mouth puckered because the lemon was _____ **sour** _____
   sweet (sour) wet

10. We need new tires because these are _____ **worn** _____
    black thick (worn)

Just for Fun! Write to show what happened next.
He put in too much air in the big balloon.

Page 68

Answer Key

Write a word from the Word Box to complete each sentence.

Word Box

late	forgot	dark	broken
young	excited	hurt	defrost

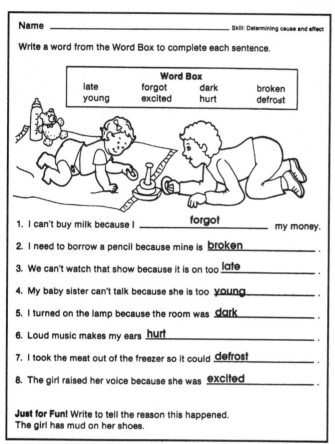

1. I can't buy milk because I **forgot** my money.

2. I need to borrow a pencil because mine is **broken** .

3. We can't watch that show because it is on too **late** .

4. My baby sister can't talk because she is too **young** .

5. I turned on the lamp because the room was **dark** .

6. Loud music makes my ears **hurt** .

7. I took the meat out of the freezer so it could **defrost** .

8. The girl raised her voice because she was **excited** .

Just for Fun! Write to tell the reason this happened.
The girl has mud on her shoes.

Page 69

Write a phrase from the Word Box to complete each sentence.

Word Box

I feed them	lemon was sour
hear the music	it was dawn
hands get clean	it was ripe
it was empty	it had stopped

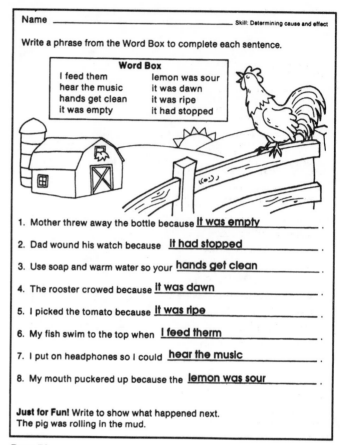

1. Mother threw away the bottle because **it was empty** .

2. Dad wound his watch because **it had stopped** .

3. Use soap and warm water so your **hands get clean** .

4. The rooster crowed because **it was dawn** .

5. I picked the tomato because **it was ripe** .

6. My fish swim to the top when **I feed them** .

7. I put on headphones so I could **hear the music** .

8. My mouth puckered up because the **lemon was sour** .

Just for Fun! Write to show what happened next.
The pig was rolling in the mud.

Page 70

Circle the correct word.
Then write the word on the line
to complete each sentence.

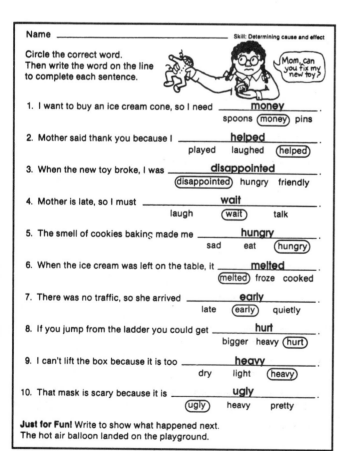

1. I want to buy an ice cream cone, so I need **money** .
spoons (money) pins

2. Mother said thank you because I **helped** .
played laughed (helped)

3. When the new toy broke, I was **disappointed** .
(disappointed) hungry friendly

4. Mother is late, so I must **wait** .
laugh (wait) talk

5. The smell of cookies baking made me **hungry** .
sad eat (hungry)

6. When the ice cream was left on the table, it **melted** .
(melted) froze cooked

7. There was no traffic, so she arrived **early** .
late (early) quietly

8. If you jump from the ladder you could get **hurt** .
bigger heavy (hurt)

9. I can't lift the box because it is too **heavy** .
dry light (heavy)

10. That mask is scary because it is **ugly** .
(ugly) heavy pretty

Just for Fun! Write to show what happened next.
The hot air balloon landed on the playground.

Page 71

So...

Write a phrase from the box at the right to tell what *most likely* happened
as a result of the action.

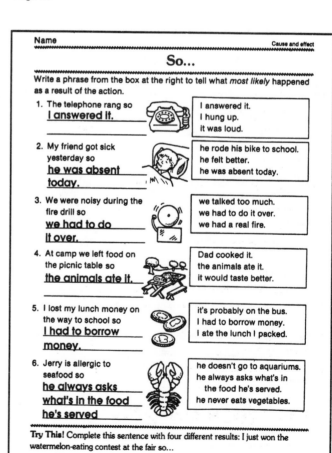

1. The telephone rang so **I answered it.**

    I answered it.
    I hung up.
    it was loud.

2. My friend got sick yesterday so **he was absent today.**

    he rode his bike to school.
    he felt better.
    he was absent today.

3. We were noisy during the fire drill so **we had to do it over.**

    we talked too much.
    we had to do it over.
    we had a real fire.

4. At camp we left food on the picnic table so **the animals ate it.**

    Dad cooked it.
    the animals ate it.
    it would taste better.

5. I lost my lunch money on the way to school so **I had to borrow money.**

    it's probably on the bus.
    I had to borrow money.
    I ate the lunch I packed.

6. Jerry is allergic to seafood so **he always asks what's in the food he's served**

    he doesn't go to aquariums.
    he always asks what's in the food he's served.
    he never eats vegetables.

Try This! Complete this sentence with four different results: I just won the
watermelon-eating contest at the fair so...

Page 72

Answer Key

Name _____ Date _____

Swimming Champ

If insects had Olympic Games, the backswimmer would be the champ. It could easily win all the swimming medals.

Backswimmers are water bugs that live in ponds. They spend all their lives on their backs. Their back legs are twice as long as their front legs. The back legs are used as paddles. Backswimmers can swim very fast. Whenever they are in danger, they swim to the bottom. They can hardly walk on land but they are good fliers.

Backswimmers can stay under the water for a long time. When they need air, they stick out their stomachs. Air flows in and is trapped in the stomach hairs. It forms a small air bubble. Then the backswimmer swims under the water again. A backswimmer's bite is deadly to other insects and small fish. It has poison in it. The bite won't kill a person but is very painful.

1. Who do backswimmers kill with their bite?
   insects and small fish

2. What part of their bodies do they use for swimming? their back legs

3. Where do backswimmers live? in ponds

4. When do backswimmers swim to the bottom? when there is danger

5. Why don't backswimmers spend much time on land? They can hardly move on land.

6. How do backswimmers breathe under water? with air bubbles in their stomachs

Brainwork! Think about the question. Write the answer on the back. Imagine you were holding an Animal Olympics. List the animals you would enter.

Page 73

Name _____ Date _____

The Walking Stick

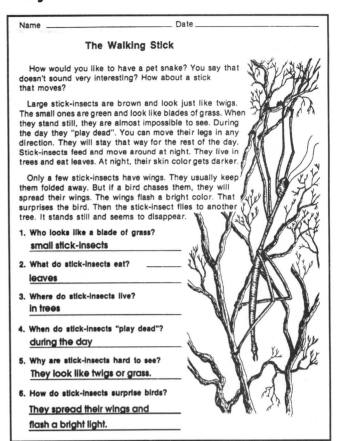

How would you like to have a pet snake? You say that doesn't sound very interesting? How about a stick that moves?

Large stick-insects are brown and look just like twigs. The small ones are green and look like blades of grass. When they stand still, they are almost impossible to see. During the day they "play dead". You can move their legs in any direction. They will stay that way for the rest of the day. Stick-insects feed and move around at night. They live in trees and eat leaves. At night, their skin color gets darker.

Only a few stick-insects have wings. They usually keep them folded away. But if a bird chases them, they will spread their wings. The wings flash a bright color. That surprises the bird. Then the stick-insect flies to another tree. It stands still and seems to disappear.

1. Who looks like a blade of grass?
   small stick-insects

2. What do stick-insects eat?
   leaves

3. Where do stick-insects live?
   in trees

4. When do stick-insects "play dead"?
   during the day

5. Why are stick-insects hard to see?
   They look like twigs or grass.

6. How do stick-insects surprise birds?
   They spread their wings and flash a bright light.

Page 74

Name _____ Date _____

Flying Ghosts

Did you ever see a ghost that looked like a bird? In South America, some people are afraid of the oilbird. They think the bird's call sounds like a dead man crying.

Oilbirds spend all their lives in darkness. During the day they live in dark caves. Not one ray of light shines through. The oilbird's legs are too weak to stand on. Instead, they hang onto the walls of the caves. They fly back and forth without bumping into the walls. As they fly, they make a clicking sound. The sound bounces off the walls. The bird can "hear" where the walls are. Once a scientist put some cotton in an oilbird's ears. The bird became helpless and crashed into the walls. When the cotton was taken out, the bird didn't hit the walls once.

Oilbirds fly out of their caves at night. They will fly up to 50 miles in search of fruit, their favorite food.

1. Who put the cotton in the oilbird's ears?
   a scientist

2. What do some people think the oilbird sounds like? a dead man crying

3. Where do oilbirds live?
   in caves in South America

4. When do oilbirds leave their caves?
   at night

5. Why is an oilbird's hearing so important?
   It hears where it's going.

6. How far will an oilbird travel for food?
   50 miles

Brainwork! Think about the question. Write the answer on the back. How do people who cannot see get around without bumping into things?

Page 75

Name _____ Date _____

Mermaids or Monsters?

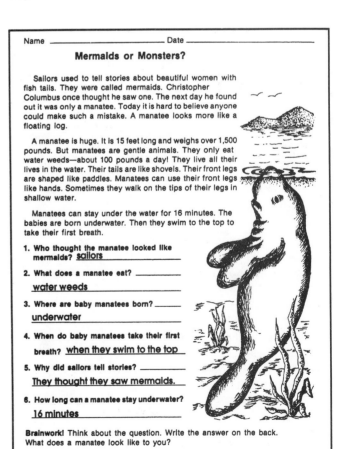

Sailors used to tell stories about beautiful women with fish tails. They were called mermaids. Christopher Columbus once thought he saw one. The next day he found out it was only a manatee. Today it is hard to believe anyone could make such a mistake. A manatee looks more like a floating log.

A manatee is huge. It is 15 feet long and weighs over 1,500 pounds. But manatees are gentle animals. They only eat water weeds—about 100 pounds a day! They live all their lives in the water. Their tails are like shovels. Their front legs are shaped like paddles. Manatees can use their front legs like hands. Sometimes they walk on the tips of their legs in shallow water.

Manatees can stay under the water for 16 minutes. The babies are born underwater. Then they swim to the top to take their first breath.

1. Who thought the manatee looked like mermaids? sailors

2. What does a manatee eat?
   water weeds

3. Where are baby manatees born?
   underwater

4. When do baby manatees take their first breath? when they swim to the top

5. Why did sailors tell stories?
   They thought they saw mermaids.

6. How long can a manatee stay underwater?
   16 minutes

Brainwork! Think about the question. Write the answer on the back. What does a manatee look like to you?

Page 76

FS-32028 Critical Thinking

Answer Key

Name _____ Date _____

Laughing Bird

If kookaburras went to school, they would probably always be in trouble. These birds never seem to stop making noise. The kookaburras laugh, scream and even bark. They usually call out at dawn or sunset. For that reason, some people call them clockbirds.

The kookaburra lives in Australia. It lives in the forest in small groups. Kookaburras are very friendly. They will accept food from people. Sometimes they even tap on windows to be fed. Kookaburras eat insects, crabs, fish and small birds. They are also quite famous as snake killers. A kookaburra will grab a snake behind its head. Then the kookaburra flies up very high and drops the snake. Kookaburras are sometimes very rude. Once a man riding through the forest fell off his horse. Two kookaburras in a nearby tree began to laugh very loudly.

1. Who made the two kookaburras laugh?
   a man who fell off his horse

2. What do kookaburras eat?
   insects, crabs, fish, small birds

3. Where do kookaburras live?
   in the forests of Australia

4. When do kookaburras call out?
   sunset and dawn

5. Why are kookaburras friendly to people?
   They want food.

6. How do kookaburras catch snakes?
   by grabbing them behind the head

Brainwork! Think about the question. Write the answer on the back. What would be some of the problems of having a kookaburra?

Page 77

Name _____ Date _____

Super Mom

The Surinam toad is the Super Mom of the animal world. What other animal would carry 60 kids on her back for four months?

The Surinam toad is only four inches long. Its flat body looks like a square pancake. Its head is shaped like a triangle. It has no tongue or teeth. This toad has touch organs on its fingers. These organs help the toad find food even in black mud. The toad uses its front feet to catch food. Then it pushes the food into its mouth. Surinam toads are strong swimmers. They spend most of their lives in water.

Just before the female lays her eggs, her skin becomes very soft. As she lays her eggs, she turns over in the water. The eggs sink into her back. The skin swells and a hole forms around each egg. Then a lid closes over each egg. After four months the lids open. The young toads swim out into the new world.

1. Who lives on the Surinam toad's back?
   baby toads

2. What does the Surinam toad use to find food?
   touch organs

3. Where does the Surinam toad live?
   In the water

4. When does a female toad's skin become soft?
   just before she lays her eggs

5. Why does the female turn over in the water?
   so the eggs will sink into her back

6. How long is a Surinam toad?
   four inches long

Brainwork! Think about the question. Write the answer on the back. What would happen to the baby toads if they weren't carried on their mother's back?

Page 78

Name _____ Date _____

Walking on Water

Basilisk lizards know a great trick. They can walk on water! The basilisk is found in South America and Mexico. In Mexico, these amazing animals are called "river runners". The male basilisk has a crest of skin on top. The crest goes from its head down to its back. Its toes are covered with small scales.

Basilisks live in bushes and trees near water. When they are frightened by another animal, they drop into the water. Sometimes they go straight down to the bottom. Other times they start running very quickly across the water. They run so fast they don't sink down. After running several feet, they slow down and begin swimming. The lizard's weight and scaly feet may keep it from sinking down.

Basilisks lay 20 eggs at a time. Afterwards, they cover the eggs with soil and leaves. The eggs hatch in three months. You can usually tell when a basilisk is relaxed. It wags its tail like a dog.

1. Who has a crest of skin on top?
   a male basilisk

2. What does the basilisk have on its toes?
   scales

3. Where does the basilisk live? In bushes
   and trees in South America and Mexico

4. When does a basilisk drop into the water?
   when it is frightened

5. Why is the basilisk so amazing?
   It walks on water.

6. How many eggs does a basilisk lay?
   20 eggs at a time

Brainwork! Think about the question. Write the answer on the back. Why can't people walk on water?

Page 79

Name _____ Date _____

Gecko in the House

Would you like a dinner guest who climbed the walls? No way, you say! In that case, don't invite a gecko!

Geckos are small lizards. They live in warm countries. Tree geckos seem to enjoy living in people's houses. Many people like geckos because they eat all the insects in the house. A gecko will go anywhere for a meal, even the ceiling! They have small hooks on the bottoms of their toes. Some geckos also have hooks on their tails. The hooks allow the gecko to climb even up glass walls. To unhook themselves, geckos curl and uncurl their toes. They can do this faster than an eye blinks.

Geckos can throw off their tails and grow new ones. Sometimes only part of the tail is thrown off. As a new tail grows, the old one heals. There have been two-tailed and even three-tailed geckos!

1. Who can climb up your walls?
   geckos

2. What do geckos eat? insects

3. Where do geckos like to live?
   in houses

4. When do geckos climb up walls?
   when looking for food

5. Why do people like geckos?
   they eat insects in the house.

6. How do geckos climb up walls?
   with hooks on their feet

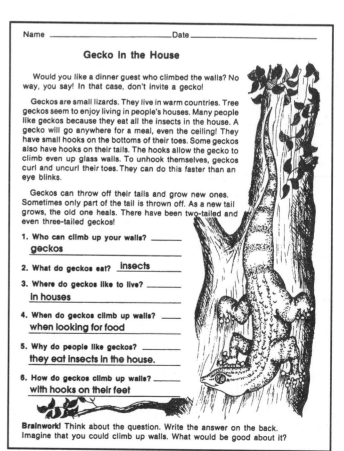

Brainwork! Think about the question. Write the answer on the back. Imagine that you could climb up walls. What would be good about it?

Page 80

Answer Key

Page 83

Eyeglasses for a Tapir

Some people think the tapir needs glasses. It is always bumping into things. Tapirs, however, can see very well. They just never look where they are going. Tapirs have escape paths marked off in the bushes. When a tiger chases them, tapirs run away without looking in front of them. Once a tapir crashed right into a canoe.

Tapirs are found in South America and Asia. They live near lakes, streams or ponds. They are good swimmers and love taking mud baths.

When baby tapirs are born they are covered with spots and stripes. These markings disappear as the animals grow. The most important part of the tapir's body is its trunk. It uses its trunk to sniff out food. Scientists think the trunk may often save the tapir's life. It may be able to smell dangerous animals before they get too close.

1. Who can scare a tapir? _tigers_
2. What is the most important part of the tapir's body? _its trunk_
3. Where do tapirs live? _near water in South America and Asia_
4. Where are tapirs covered with stripes and spots? _when they are born_
5. Why do tapirs always bump into things? _They don't look where they are going._
6. How do tapirs protect themselves from dangerous animals? _They run them down escape paths._

Brainwork! Think about the question. Write the answer on the back. Which sense is the most important to you: smell, taste, sight, hearing or touch? Why?

Page 86

Mr. Mole's Fruit Mart

Read each sentence. Can you tell if it is a fact by looking at the picture? If you can, write FACT. If you cannot tell by just looking at the picture, write DON'T KNOW.

1. The apples are on sale. _fact_
2. The store belongs to Mr. Mole. _fact_
3. The melons are the largest fruit. _don't know_
4. The pears are ripe. _don't know_
5. There are two kinds of peaches. _fact_
6. Mr. Mole is a father. _don't know_
7. There is a scale. _fact_
8. The fruit was picked yesterday. _don't know_

Answer these questions with a fact.

9. How much do pears cost? _25¢ a pound_
10. Where is Mr. Mole's hand? _on the apples_
11. Where are the lemons from? _Florida_

★ Why do you think the apples are on sale?

Page 82

Deadly Snake

Many strange stories are told about the anaconda snake. Some people say it turns into a ship with sails at night. Others believe that the anaconda can swallow a man in one gulp.

Most of these stories are just tall tales. However, the anaconda really is one of the world's most dangerous animals. It is the largest of all snakes. The longest anaconda ever found was 37 feet long! Anacondas live in South America.

During the day these snakes sleep in tree branches. They move slowly on land. Anacondas can swim very quickly. They wait for an animal to come near the water's edge. Then they wind themselves around its body and drag it into the water. They hold the animal under the water until it drowns. Then they swallow the animal whole. Anacondas eat birds, fish, deer and even alligators. After a big meal, an anaconda snake will not move for a week.

1. Who can swallow an alligator whole? _an anaconda_
2. What did some people think an anaconda turned into at night? _ships with sails_
3. Where do anacondas catch their dinners? _near the water's edge_
4. When do anacondas sleep? _in the daytime_
5. Why are people afraid of anacondas? _They think an anaconda can swallow them._
6. How long will an anaconda rest after one meal? _one week_

Brainwork! Think about the question. Write the answer on the back. Write a one-paragraph story about an anaconda.

Page 85

The Biggest One of All

If you ever saw a 120-pound rat, you'd probably be scared. Don't worry. The capybara is not really a rat. Both the capybara and the rat are rodents. The capybara, however, is harmless. Some capybaras have even been trained as pets.

The capybara is the world's largest rodent. It's four feet long. It has reddish-brown hair and small eyes and ears. This animal lives in South America. It eats water plants and grass.

Capybaras are super swimmers. Their feet are webbed like ducks' feet. They dive and swim far distances under water. When they are frightened, they will run like horses. Then they will jump into the nearest river. When they swim under water, only their eyes, ears and noses show. Capybaras can't stay out of water too long. If they do, their skin dries out. Since they like water so much, capybaras are sometimes called water pigs.

1. What do capybaras look like? _rats_
2. What do capybaras eat? _water plants and grass_
3. Where are capybaras found? _in South America_
4. When do capybaras run like horses? _when they are frightened_
5. Why must capybaras live near water? _so their skin won't dry out_
6. How much do capybaras weigh? _120 pounds_

Brainwork! Think about the question. Write the answer on the back. Do you think a capybara would make a good pet? Why or why not?

Page 81

A Snaky Animal

It has a long, skinny neck that moves from side to side. When it finds something to eat, it strikes out. Then it swallows the dinner in one gulp. It's a snake, right? No, it's a turtle!

Snake-necked turtles are probably the world's strangest looking turtles. They live in South America and Australia. Their necks are sometimes as long as their bodies! Most of them cannot put their necks inside their shells. They just wrap their necks around their shells.

The snake-necked turtle lives in fresh water. It can swim underwater for a long time. To breathe, it keeps its nose just above the water. These turtles eat fish.

One kind of snake-necked turtle is called the "stinker". When it gets upset, it gives off a rotten smell. You can be sure that other animals leave the stinker alone.

1. Who gives off a bad smell? _the stinker turtle_
2. What kind of neck does a snake-necked turtle have? _a long one_
3. Where do snake-necked turtles live? _in the water in South America and Australia_
4. When does the snake-necked turtle strike out with its neck? _when it finds food_
5. Why can't these turtles put their necks inside their shells? _Their necks are too long._
6. How does this turtle breathe underwater? _It keeps its nose above water._

Brainwork! Think about the question. Write the answer on the back. Make a list of at least five animals that have long necks.

Page 84

Life Upside Down

Would you like to spend your whole life upside-down? Well, the sloth seems to enjoy it. The sloth eats, sleeps and moves upside-down. It lives in the treetops of South America. It hangs onto branches with its long, sharp claws.

Everything about the sloth seems to be backwards. Even its hair grows backwards. The sloth can turn its head almost all the way around! It can raise its head up, while its body hangs down. The sloth hardly ever moves. When it does, it only goes one-third mile per hour. Some sloths live their entire lives in one tree! They eat fruits and leaves from the tree. Baby sloths are born upside-down. They hang onto their mother's stomach until they get big. Then they slowly move to another branch. Sloth mothers don't worry about the kids moving too far from home.

1. Who carries sloth babies on her stomach? _a mother sloth_
2. What do sloths eat? _fruits and leaves from trees_
3. Where do sloths hang? _in trees_
4. When do sloths hang upside-down? _all their lives_
5. Why do sloths have long, sharp claws? _so they can hang from the branches of trees_
6. How far can a sloth turn its head? _almost all the way around_

Brainwork! Think about the question. Write the answer on the back. Sometimes people are called "slothful". What do you think that means?

Answer Key

Page 87

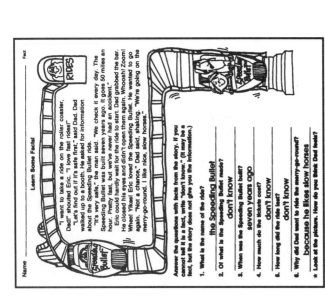

Name _____

Learn Some Facts!

"I want to take a ride on the roller coaster, Dad!" shouted Eric. "I love fast rides!"

"Let's find out if it's safe first," said Dad. Dad walked up to a booth. He asked for information about the Speeding Bullet ride.

"It's very safe," the man said. "We check it every day. The Speeding Bullet was built seven years ago. It goes 50 miles an hour. Pretty fast, but we've never had an accident."

Eric could hardly wait for the ride to start. Dad grabbed the bar. He closed his eyes and didn't open them again. Whoosh! Zoom! Wheel Yikes! Eric loved the Speeding Bullet. He wanted to go again. "Not a chance," Dad said, shaking. "We're going on the merry-go-round. I like nice, slow horses."

Answer the questions with facts from the story. If you cannot tell if it is a fact, write "don't know." (It may be a fact, but the story does not give you the information.)

1. What is the name of the ride?
   the Speeding Bullet

2. Of what is the Speeding Bullet made?
   don't know

3. When was the Speeding Bullet built?
   seven years ago

4. How much do the tickets cost?
   don't know

5. How long did the ride last?
   don't know

6. Why did Dad want to ride to the merry-go-round?
   because he likes slow horses

★ Look at the picture. How do you think Dad feels?

Page 88

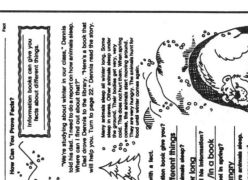

Name _____

Newspapers can give you the facts of a story.

Where Are The Facts?
Children Want Park
by Rich Andrews

Early Monday morning, 50 children marched into the mayor's office. "We need a place to play!" they all said.

"There is no empty land to build a park," answered the mayor. "But let me talk to my friends. Maybe we can think of something for you." Two weeks went by. The children had to play on the sidewalks. It was too crowded to even throw a ball.

Late one night, David Lopez heard something outside his window. He saw some men putting up fences across each end of the street. They hung up a sign: "CHILDREN'S PARK—NO CARS ALLOWED". At last, the children had a place to play.

If the sentence is a fact, write FACT. If it is not a fact stated in the story, write DK ("don't know").

1. All sidewalks are crowded. ___dk___

2. David Lopez can sing. ___dk___

3. The children wanted a park. ___fact___

4. Some men put up a fence. ___fact___

5. There is no empty land. ___fact___

6. A sign said, "CHILDREN'S PARK". ___fact___

7. Why did the children want a park?
   They needed a place to play.

8. When did the children go see the park?
   early Monday morning

★ Where do you think all the children lived?

Page 89

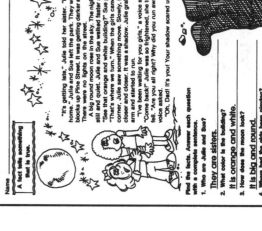

Name _____

Check for Facts

Read each sentence. If it is a fact, write F. Check the story. Some questions you cannot answer. There are not enough facts. Write DK ("don't know") on the line.

1. Peter is president of the club. ___dk___
2. Fred is not a club member. ___f___
3. The meeting is on Tuesday. ___dk___
4. Only boys belong to the club. ___dk___
5. Fred lives at 6320 Clock Lane. ___f___
6. Peter is smarter than Chuck. ___dk___
7. Why do you think Fred is not a member of the club?

Page 90

Name _____

A fact tells something that is true. You can prove it.

Look at each picture carefully. If a sentence is a fact, write FACT. You must prove it by looking at the picture. If you cannot prove the sentence is a fact, write DK ("don't know").

1. Sarah is talking on the phone. ___fact___
2. The phone is on the table. ___fact___
3. The man is Sarah's father. ___dk___
4. A note is on the desk. ___fact___
5. The man is very tall. ___dk___
6. The man bought his pen. ___dk___

7. "It has flowers on it" would be a fact about: __Sarah's bed__

8. "It is a fruit" would be a fact about: __the apple__

9. Write a fact about Sarah: __Answers vary__

10. Write a fact about the clock: __Answers vary__

11. "It is broken" is a fact about: __the pencil__

12. Write a fact about the man's suit: __Answers vary__

★ What do you think Sarah is talking about?

Page 91

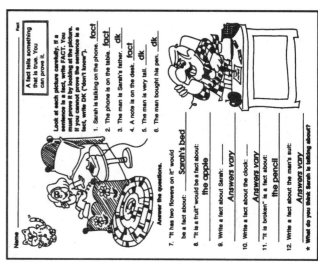

Name _____

How Can You Prove Facts?

Information books can give you facts about different things.

"We're studying about winter in our class," Dennis told his dad. "I need to do a report on how animals sleep. Where can I find out about that?"

Dad drove Dennis to the library. "Here's a book that will help you. Turn to page 22," Dennis read the story.

Many animals sleep all winter long. Some sleep in caves. Other animals sleep under the ground. Their bodies get very, very cold. This does not hurt them. When spring comes, the animals start moving around. They are very hungry. The animals hunt for food until winter comes again.

Answer each question with a fact.

1. What does an information book give you?
   facts about different things

2. How long do many animals sleep?
   all winter long

3. Where did Dennis find his information?
   of the library /in a book

4. How do the animals feel in spring?
   very hungry

5. Name two places where animals sleep.
   caves, underground

6. Write two facts about the picture above.
   Answers vary

★ What do you think is the most interesting part of the animal story?

Page 92

Name _____

A fact tells something that is true.

"It's getting late," Julie told her sister. "Let's hurry home." Julie and Sue left the park. They walked four blocks up Pine Street. It was getting darker and darker. The night was very still and quiet. There were no lights on the street. A big round moon rose in the sky.

"See that orange and white building?" Sue pointed. "That's where we turn." When the girls came to the corner, Julie saw something move. Slowly, it came closer and closer. It was a shadow. Julie grabbed Sue's arm and started to run.

"Come back!" Julie was so frightened, she tripped and fell. "Are you all right? Why did you run away?" the voice asked.

"Oh, Dad! It's you! Your shadow scared us!"

Find the facts. Answer each question with a complete sentence.

1. Who are Julie and Sue?
   They are sisters.

2. What color is the building?
   It is orange and white.

3. How does the moon look?
   It is big and round.

4. Where had the girls been playing?
   They were playing in the park.

5. On what street did the girls walk?
   They walked up Pine Street.

★ Look at the picture. Why does a shadow seem very scary?

126

FS-32028 Critical Thinking

Answer Key

Page 95

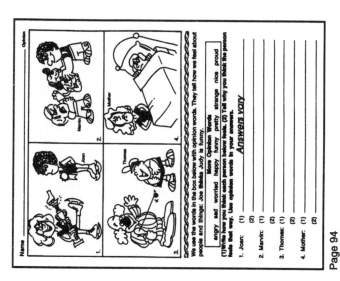

Page 94

Page 93

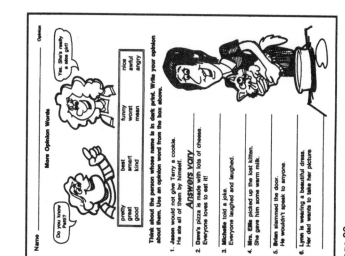

Page 98

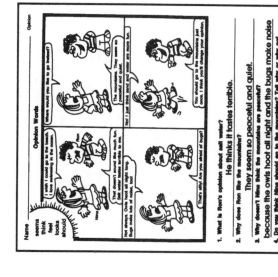

Page 97

Page 96

127

Answer Key

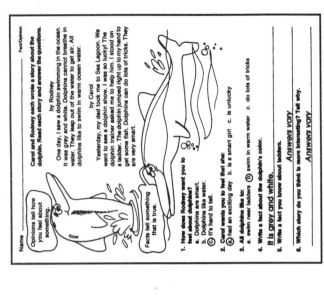

Page 101

Carol and Rodney each wrote a story about the dolphin. Read each story and answer the questions.

Opinions tell how you feel about something.

Facts tell something that is true.

by Rodney
One day, I saw a dolphin swimming in the ocean. It was gray and white. Dolphins cannot breathe in water. They leap out of the water to get air. All dolphins like to swim in warm ocean water.

by Carol
Yesterday, my dad took me to Sea Lagoon. We went to see a dolphin show. I was so lucky! The dolphin trainer asked me to help him. I stood on a ladder. The dolphin jumped right up to my hand to get some fish. Dolphins can do lots of tricks. They are very smart.

1. How does Rodney want you to feel about dolphins?
   a. Dolphins are smart.
   b. Dolphins like water.
   c. It's hard to tell.
2. Carol wants you to feel that she:
   a. had an exciting day   b. is a smart girl   c. is unlucky
3. All dolphins like to:
   a. swim near ladders   b. swim in warm water   c. do lots of tricks
4. Write a fact about the dolphin's color.
   It is grey and white.
5. Write a fact you know about ladders.
   Answers vary
6. Which story do you think is more interesting? Tell why.
   Answers vary

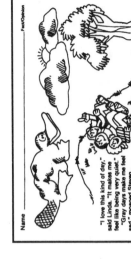

Page 104

"I love this kind of day," said Linda. "It makes me feel like being very quiet." "Gray days make me feel sad," moaned Steven, putting on a sweater. "I like warm sunny days best. They make me feel happy." "Look at that cloud over there," pointed Carol. "It has a tail and feet just like a duck, don't you think?" "It has a tail. It has a long trunk. I think it's an elephant. It's not an elephant. It's not a duck," said Linda.
Linda looked at the cloud carefully. "I think it's an elephant. It has a long trunk hanging down."
Steven stared at the cloud a long time. "I have it! It's not a duck. It's a platypus!"

Look at the picture. If the sentence is a fact, write FACT. If you cannot tell, write DK.
1. Linda likes the grass. __dk__   5. Carol has a toy. __dk__
2. The cloud has a tail. __fact__   6. There is an apple tree. __dk__
3. The children are lost. __dk__   7. Linda is wearing shoes. __fact__
4. It is November. __dk__   8. It is early morning. __dk__

Answer each question.
9. Do you think Steven is cold? How can you tell?
   Yes. He is putting on his sweater.
10. What does Linda think about the cloud?
    She thinks it looks like an elephant.
11. How does Steven feel about gray days?
    They make him feel sad.

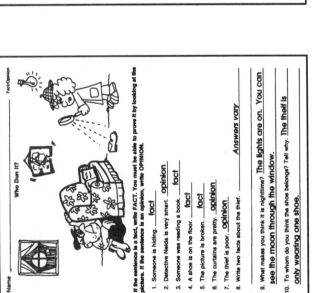

Page 100

Has anyone seen this boy? Farmer Rooney is looking for him. He thinks Barney took his prize rooster, Rocky. "Barney never, ever gets up on time for school," Farmer Rooney explained. "He is always late. That makes his teacher very angry. Barney doesn't like alarm clocks. He cock-a-doodles and he sings, too. He knows lots of songs—Twinkle Little Star, Row Your Boat. I sure miss ol' Rocky. H-m-m-m. I've got an idea. I'll put Rocky's voice on tape. Barney can put the tape inside his clock. Then we'll both get up on time!"

WANTED BARNEY O'MALLEY

Description of Barney O'Malley
Eyes: Brown
Hair: Red
Height: Five feet
Age: 12 years

If the sentence is a fact, write FACT. If it is an opinion, write OPINION.
1. Rocky is a rooster. __fact__
2. Farmer Rooney is sad. __opinion__
3. Barney's teacher is nice. __fact__
4. Some clocks have alarms. __fact__
5. Rocky is a very good singer. __opinion__
6. Barney has red hair. __fact__
7. Barney is always late. __fact__

Answer each question.
8. Do you think Farmer Rooney has a clock? Tell why or why not.
   Answers vary
9. How does Barney feel about alarms? Tell why.
   He does not like them. He wakes up feeling crabby.
10. Why do you think Barney has such a hard time waking up?
    Answers vary

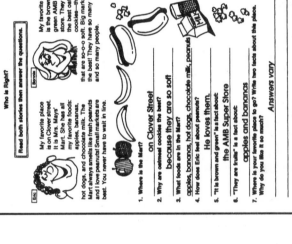

Page 103

Who is Right?
Read both stories then answer the questions.

Eric: My favorite place is on Clover street. It is Mrs. May's Mart. She has all my favorite foods: apples, bananas, hot dogs, and chocolate milk. The Mart always smells like fresh peanuts and I love peanuts! Small markets are best. You never have to wait in line.

Bonnie: My favorite place is the brown and green AMB super store. They have the best oatmeal cookies—the kind that are so-o-o soft. Big markets are the best! They have so many foods and so many people.

1. Where is the Mart?
   on Clover Street
2. Why are oatmeal cookies the best?
   because they are so soft
3. What foods are in the Mart?
   apples, bananas, hot dogs, chocolate milk, peanuts
4. How does Eric feel about peanuts?
   He loves them.
5. "It is brown and green" is a fact about:
   the AMB Super Store
6. "They are fruits" is a fact about:
   apples and bananas
7. Where is your favorite place to go? Write two facts about the place. Why do you like it so much?
   Answers vary

Page 99

Who Dun It?

If the sentence is a fact, write FACT. You must be able to prove it by looking at the picture. If the sentence is an opinion, write OPINION.
1. Someone is hiding. __fact__
2. Detective Nelda is very smart. __opinion__
3. Someone was reading a book. __fact__
4. A shoe is on the floor. __fact__
5. The picture is broken. __fact__
6. The curtains are pretty. __opinion__
7. The thief is poor. __opinion__
8. Write two facts about the thief.
   Answers vary
9. What makes you think it is nighttime? The lights are on. You can see the moon through the window.
10. To whom do you think the shoe belongs? Tell why. The thief is only wearing one shoe.

Page 102

"Do you want to taste something really special? Try Razzle-Dazzle Bubble Gum—the gum with zap! and zing! It'll wake up your mouth. Razzle-Dazzle comes in four flavors: cherry, grape, tooty-frooty, and red hot pepper. As I unwrap the paper, I can smell those peppers! Sniff M-m-m-m!
"Now, here's the surprise. You can blow square bubbles with Razzle-Dazzle. (Chew, chew, chew. Phoo, phoo, POP!) Isn't that terrific? I think blowing bubbles is more fun than anything!
"Rush out now and buy some Razzle-Dazzle. Each pack costs 25 cents. One little piece will make you feel like a new person. Hurry!"

Ads can tell facts and opinions.

Write whether each sentence is a FACT or Percy's OPINION.
1. Razzle-Dazzle is a gum. __fact__
2. Razzle-Dazzle comes in four flavors. __fact__
3. Red hot pepper is the best flavor. __opinion__
4. Razzle-Dazzle has zing! __opinion__
5. Razzle-Dazzle costs 25 cents. __fact__
6. Blowing bubbles is fun! __opinion__
7. What do you think of Percy's clothes?
   Answers vary
8. Would you buy Razzle-Dazzle Gum? Tell why or why not.
   Answers vary
9. What is your favorite food? Tell me why I should like it.
   Answers vary

FS-32028 Critical Thinking